GLOBETROTTER
TRAVEL ATLAS

Road Atlas of
SOUTH AFRICA

NEW
HOLLAND

National Route Planner

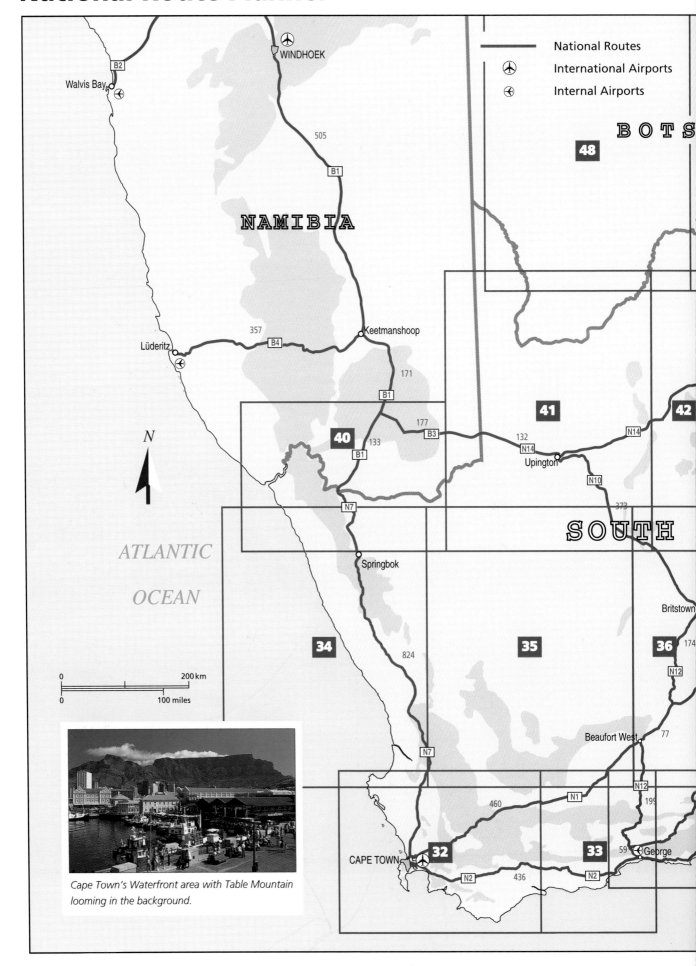

National Routes

⊕ International Airports

✈ Internal Airports

BOTS

48

WINDHOEK

Walvis Bay

B2

505

B1

NAMIBIA

357

Keetmanshoop

B4

Lüderitz

171

B1

N

177

B3

132

N14

41

42

133

N14

B1

40

Upington

N10

N7

373

SOUTH

ATLANTIC

Springbok

OCEAN

0   200 km

0   100 miles

34

35

36   174

N12

Britstown

Beaufort West   77

N7

N12

N1

460

199

CAPE TOWN

32

33   59   George

N2

436

N2

Cape Town's Waterfront area with Table Mountain looming in the background.

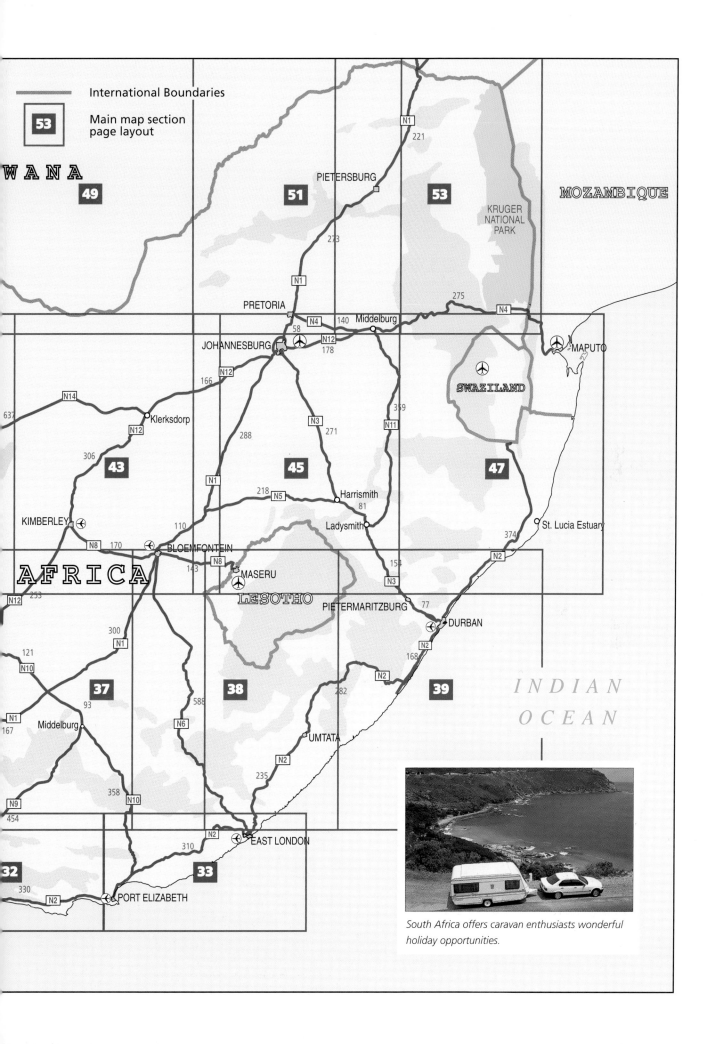

International Boundaries

53 Main map section
page layout

WANA

49

51

PIETERSBURG

53

MOZAMBIQUE

221

N1

KRUGER
NATIONAL
PARK

273

N1

275

PRETORIA

N4

N4

MAPUTO

58

N4

140

Middelburg

JOHANNESBURG

N12

178

SWAZILAND

N12

166

359

N14

N11

637

N12

43

288

N3

271

306

Klerksdorp

47

110

KIMBERLEY

N1

45

218

N5

Harrismith

81

Ladysmith

St. Lucia Estuary

N8

170

BLOEMFONTEIN

374

N8

AFRICA

143

154

N2

MASERU

N3

N12

253

LESOTHO

PIETERMARITZBURG

77

300

N1

DURBAN

121

588

N2

N10

282

168

INDIAN

37

38

N2

39

93

N6

OCEAN

N1

167

Middelburg

UMTATA

358

N2

N10

235

N9

454

N2

EAST LONDON

32

33

310

330

N2

PORT ELIZABETH

*South Africa offers caravan enthusiasts wonderful
holiday opportunities.*

Key Tourist Areas

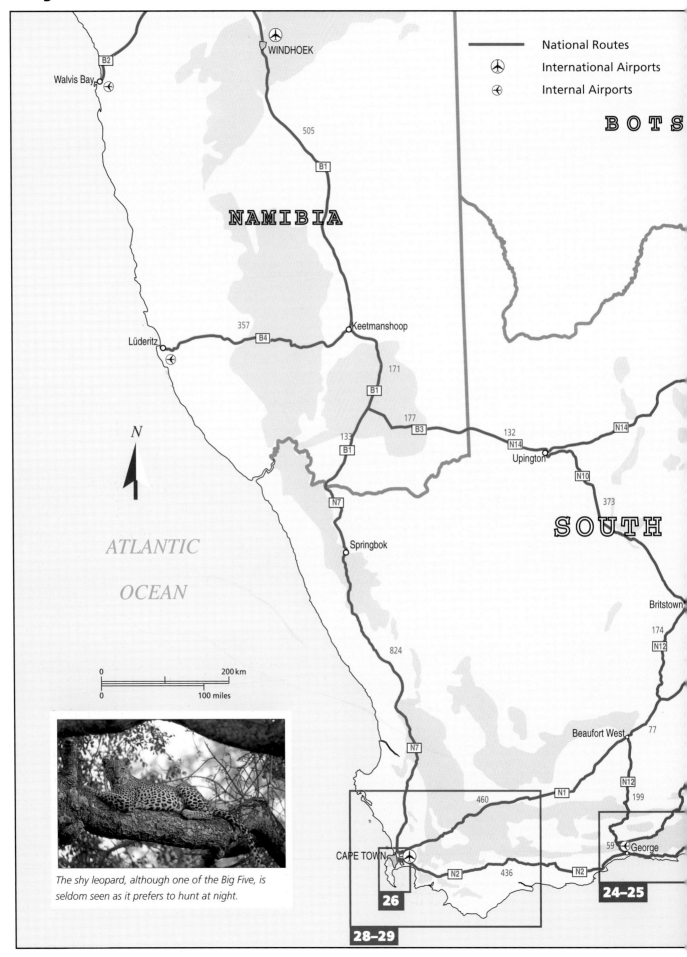

National Routes

✈ International Airports

✈ Internal Airports

WINDHOEK

Walvis Bay

B2

505

B1

NAMIBIA

BOTS

357

Lüderitz

B4

Keetmanshoop

171

B1

177

133

B3

132

N14

N14

B1

Upington

N10

N7

373

SOUTH

N

ATLANTIC

OCEAN

Springbok

824

Britstown

174

N12

200 km

100 miles

Beaufort West

77

N7

N12

199

N1

460

Britstown

N2

436

N2

59 ✈ George

CAPE TOWN ✈

N2

26

28–29

24–25

The shy leopard, although one of the Big Five, is seldom seen as it prefers to hunt at night.

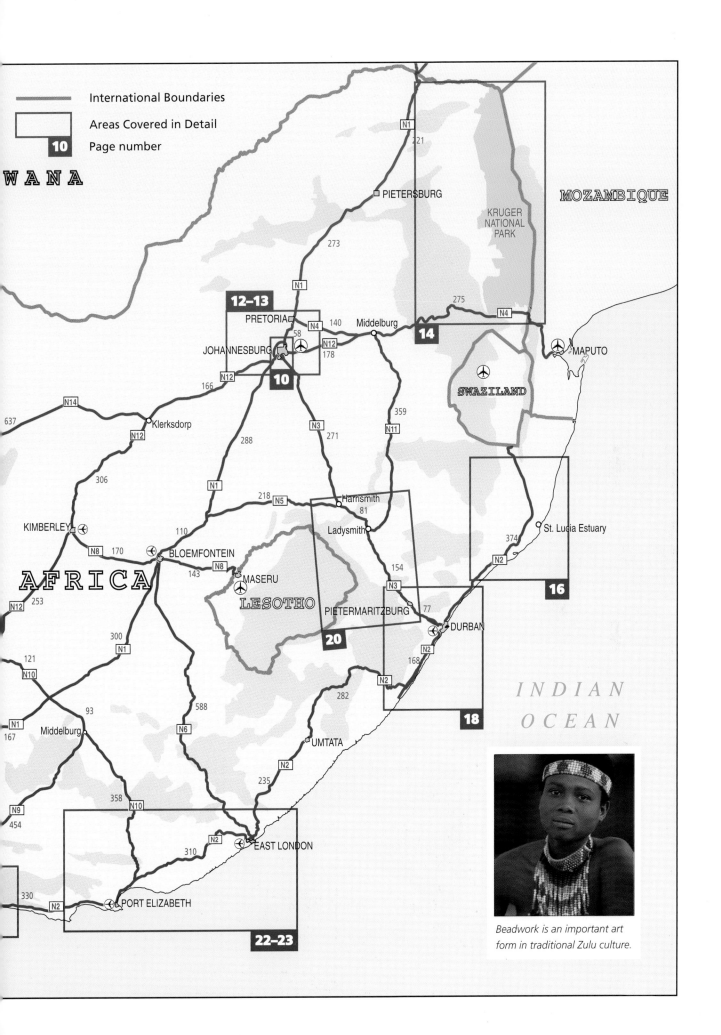

10

12–13

14

16

20

18

22–23

International Boundaries

Areas Covered in Detail

10 Page number

WANA

MOZAMBIQUE

PIETERSBURG

KRUGER
NATIONAL
PARK

N1

221

273

N1

PRETORIA

JOHANNESBURG

N4 140 Middelburg

58

N12

178

N12

166

N14

637

Klerksdorp

N12

306

N1

288

N3 271

359

N11

MAPUTO

SWAZILAND

St. Lucia Estuary

374

N2

KIMBERLEY

AFRICA

N8 170

BLOEMFONTEIN

143 N8

MASERU

LESOTHO

218 N5

110

Harrismith

81

Ladysmith

PIETERMARITZBURG

154

N3

N2

N12 253

300 N1

121

N10

93

N6

588

Middelburg

N1

167

N9

454

358 N10

N2

310

EAST LONDON

330

N2

PORT ELIZABETH

235

N2

282

UMTATA

77

DURBAN

N2

168

N2

INDIAN

OCEAN

*Beadwork is an important art
form in traditional Zulu culture.*

Published in 1994 by
New Holland (Publishers) Ltd
London • Cape Town • Sydney

Copyright © 1994 in text: New Holland
(Publishers) Ltd
Copyright © 1994 in maps: New Holland
(Publishers) Ltd
Copyright © 1994 in photographs:
Individual photographers and Struik Image
Library as credited below
Copyright © 1994 New Holland
(Publishers) Ltd

ISBN 1 85368 393 0

New Holland (Publishers) Ltd
37 Connaught Street, London W2 2AZ

Project coordinator: John Hall
Text: Peter Joyce
Copy editors: Vincent le Roux, Sandie Vahl
Cover design: Neville Poulter
Designer: Darren MacGurk
Cartography: Globetrotter Travel Maps
Cartographers: John Loubser, Nadine
Liebenberg, Bill Smuts
Cartographic Researcher: Estelle Cohen
Typeset by Struik DTP
Reproduction by Hirt & Carter (Pty) Ltd,
Cape Town
Printed and bound in Singapore by Tien
Wah Press (Pte) Ltd

Photographic Credits

Shaen Adey: pages 16 above, 46 below left, 63 right; **Daryl Balfour:** page 14 below right; **Gerald Cubitt:** page 67; **Roger de la Harpe:** pages 4, 5, 9, 20 above right, 61; **Nigel Dennis:** page 14 left; **Jan Frederick:** pages 26 above left [Photo Access]; **C.L. Glittens:** page 44 above right [Photo Access]; **Walter Knirr:** front cover, pages 1, 10 left, 10 right [Photo Access], 12 [Photo Access], 16 below [Photo Access], 18 left [Photo Access], 18 right [Photo Access], 20 left [Photo Access], 20 below right [Photo Access], 26 right [Photo Access], 31, 40 left [Photo Access], 40 right [Photo Access], 42, 44 left [Photo Access], 46 above left [Photo Access], 50 above left [Photo Access], 50 below left [Photo Access], 50 right , 52 left [Photo Access], 55 above, 55 below, 58, 59 [Photo Access], 60 [Photo Access], 62 [Photo Access]; **Colin Paterson-Jones:** page 46 right; **Alain Proust:** page 2; **David Steele:** page 3 [Photo Access]; **Struik Image Library:** Leonard Hoffmann pages 36, 66, Peter Pickford pages 14 above right, 34,39, 49, 52 right, Erhardt Thiel 26 below left, 63 above left; **Janek Szymanowski:** pages 33 below, 63 below left, 68; **Colin Urquhart:** page 23; **Mark van Aardt:** page 25 left; **Hein von Hörsten:** page 25 right; **Lanz von Hörsten:** pages 7, 33 above, 44 below right.

The new, brightly coloured South African flag was first raised at midnight on 26 April 1994. For many people it is a symbol of hope, as a new political era of democracy in South Africa commences.

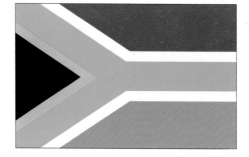

**Emergency Telephone Numbers
Notrufnummern
Appels d'Urgence**

	Telephone
Police Polizeirevier Poste de police	10111
Fire Feuerwehr Pompiers	461 4141
Ambulance Krankenwagen Ambulances	10172
Hospital Krankenhaus Hôpital	404 9111

Contents
Inhaltsverzeichnis
Sommaire

	pages
Distance, Climate and Toll Road Charts	8

Key Tourist Areas
Ausgewählte Regionalkarten
Cartes touristiques

	pages
Legend Zeichenerklärung Légende	9
Greater Johannesburg	10
Witwatersrand	12
Kruger National Park	14
KwaZulu Natal North Coast	16
KwaZulu Natal South Coast	18
Drakensberg Mountain Resorts	20
Eastern Cape	22
Garden Route	24
Cape Peninsula	26
West Coast, Cape Peninsula, Winelands and Overberg	28

Main Map Section
Gesamtdarstellung
Cartes

	pages
Key & Legend Schlüssel und Zeichenerklärung Carte générale et légende	30
Eastern and Western Cape	31
West Coast, Namaqualand & Great Karoo	34
The Great Karoo	36
KwaZulu Natal, Lesotho and Wild Coast	38
Northern Cape	40
Kimberley and Bloemfontein	42
Northeastern Orange Free State	44
Northern KwaZulu Natal	46
Botswana and North West	48
North West and Northern Transvaal	50
Eastern and Northern Transvaal	52

Town Plans
Stadtpläne
Plans des villes

	pages
Key & Legend Schlüssel und Zeichenerklärung Carte générale et légende	54
Johannesburg City Centre	55
Pretoria City Centre	58
Bloemfontein City Centre	59
Durban City Centre	60
Pietermaritzburg City Centre	61
Kimberley City Centre	62
Cape Town City Centre	63
Port Elizabeth City Centre	66
East London City Centre	67
Nelspruit Town Centre	68

	page
Place Names Index to Main Map Section	69

This elegant manor house, nestled at the foot of the majestic Groot Drakenstein mountains, is a fine example of Cape Dutch architecture. The distinctive central gable is a feature of this building style.

Distance, Climate and Toll Road Charts

APPROXIMATE DISTANCES IN KILOMETRES	BLOEMFONTEIN	CAPE TOWN	DURBAN	EAST LONDON	GABORONE	GRAHAMSTOWN	JOHANNESBURG	KIMBERLEY	MAPUTO	MASERU	MBABANE	PORT ELIZABETH	PRETORIA	WELKOM	WINDHOEK
BEAUFORT WEST	544	460	1178	605	1042	492	942	504	1349	609	1129	501	1000	697	1629
BLOEMFONTEIN		1004	634	584	622	601	398	177	897	157	677	677	456	153	1593
BRITSTOWN	398	710	1032	609	791	496	725	253	1289	555	1075	572	783	551	1378
CAPE TOWN	1004		1753	1099	1501	899	1402	962	1900	1160	1680	769	1460	1156	1500
COLESBERG	226	778	860	488	848	375	624	292	1123	383	903	451	682	379	1573
DE AAR	346	762	980	557	843	444	744	305	1243	503	1023	520	802	499	1430
DURBAN	634	1753		674	979	854	588	811	625	590	562	984	646	564	2227
EAST LONDON	584	1079	674		1206	180	982	780	1301	630	1238	310	1040	737	1987
GABORONE	622	1501	979	1206		1223	358	538	957	702	719	1299	350	479	1735
GEORGE	773	438	1319	645	1361	465	1171	762	1670	913	1450	335	1229	926	1887
GRAAFF-REINET	424	787	942	395	1012	282	822	490	1321	599	1101	291	880	577	1697
GRAHAMSTOWN	601	899	854	180	1223		999	667	1478	692	1418	130	1057	754	1856
HARRISMITH	328	1331	306	822	673	929	282	505	649	284	468	1068	332	258	1921
JOHANNESBURG	398	1402	588	982	358	999		472	599	438	361	1075	58	258	1801
KEETMANSHOOP	1088	995	1722	1482	1230	1351	1296	911	1895	1245	1657	1445	1354	1205	505
KIMBERLEY	177	962	811	780	538	667	472		1071	334	833	743	530	294	1416
KLERKSDORP	288	1271	645	872	334	889	164	308	763	368	525	1009	222	145	1693
KROONSTAD	211	1214	537	795	442	812	187	339	742	247	522	888	245	71	1724
LADYSMITH	410	1413	236	752	755	932	364	587	567	366	386	1062	422	340	2008
MAFIKENG	464	1343	821	1048	158	1065	287	380	886	544	648	1141	294	321	1577
MAPUTO	897	1900	625	1301	957	1478	599	1071		853	223	1609	583	813	2400
MASERU	157	1160	590	630	702	692	438	334	853		633	822	488	249	1750
MBABANE	677	1680	562	1238	719	1418	361	833	223	633		1548	372	451	2162
MESSINA	928	1932	1118	1512	696	1529	530	1002	725	960	808	1605	472	788	2331
NELSPRUIT	757	1762	707	1226	672	1358	355	827	244	713	173	1434	322	639	2156
OUDTSHOORN	743	506	1294	704	1241	532	1141	703	1705	959	1417	394	1199	896	1828
PIETERMARITZBURG	555	1674	79	595	900	775	509	732	706	511	640	905	567	485	2148
PIETERSBURG	717	1721	907	1301	485	1318	319	791	605	749	515	1394	261	577	2120
PORT ELIZABETH	677	769	984	310	1299	130	1075	743	1609	822	1548		1133	830	1950
PRETORIA	456	1460	646	1040	350	1057	58	530	583	488	372	1133		316	1859
QUEENSTOWN	377	1069	676	207	999	269	775	534	1302	423	1240	399	833	525	1829
UMTATA	570	1314	439	235	1192	415	869	747	1064	616	1003	545	928	718	2066
UPINGTON	588	894	1222	982	730	851	796	411	1395	745	1157	945	854	669	1005
WELKOM	153	1156	564	737	479	754	258	294	813	249	451	830	316		1679
WINDHOEK	1593	1500	2227	1987	1735	1856	1801	1416	2400	1750	2162	1950	1859	1679	

Distance Charts

In order to find out the distance between two of the country's major centres, first locate the name of the town or city on the vertical or horizontal column, then locate the name of the other town or city on the other column and, finally, read off the number where the vertical and horizontal lines intersect.

Climate Charts

Below is an example of a Climate Chart. These occur throughout the atlas, and give the average temperatures and rainfall for the relevant region or city.

JOHANNESBURG	J	F	M	A	M	J	J	A	S	O	N	D
AVERAGE TEMP. °F	68	67	65	60	55	50	51	55	61	63	65	67
AVERAGE TEMP. °C	20	20	18	16	13	10	10	13	16	18	18	19
Hours of Sun Daily	8	8	8	8	9	9	9	10	9	9	8	8
RAINFALL in	5	4	3	2	1	0.5	0.5	0.5	1	3	4	4
RAINFALL mm	131	95	81	55	19	7	6	6	26	72	114	106
Days of Rainfall	15	11	11	9	4	2	1	2	3	10	14	14

Toll Road Chart

The various provinces of South Africa are served by a number of time-saving toll roads. The chart below identifies the names of these toll roads, where the toll plaza for each is situated, the points between which the toll roads stretch and the grid references for locating these roads on the maps in this book.

ROUTE	PROVINCE	NAME	TOLL PLAZA	LOCATION	PAGE
N1	CAPE	HUGUENOT TUNNEL	MARKET STREET	DU TOITS KLOOF	30 B4
N1	OFS	KROONVAAL	VAAL	UNCLE CHARLIES-KROONSTAD	43 B2
N1	TRANSVAAL		GRASMERE		43 B1
N1	TRANSVAAL	KRANSKOP	KRANSKOP	WARMBATHS-MIDDELFONTEIN	49 C4
N2	CAPE	TSITSIKAMMA	TSITSIKAMMA	THE CRAGS & STORMS RIVER	30 B2
	NATAL	SOUTH COAST	MARBURG	SOUTHBROOM-MARBURG	37 F3
N2	NATAL	NORTH COAST	TONGAAT	UMDLOTI-BALLITO	37 G2
N3	OFS	HIGHVELD	WILGE	VILLIERS-WARDEN	43 C2
N3	NATAL	MIDLANDS	TUGELA	KEEVERSFONTEIN-FRERE	43 D4
			MOOI	FRERE-CEDARA	37 F1
N3	NATAL	MARIANNHILL	MARIANNHILL	ASSAGAY-PINETOWN	37 F2
N4	TRANSVAAL	MAGALIES	MAGALIES	PRETORIA-HARTBEESPOORT	49 B5
N17	TRANSVAAL	SPRINGS to	DALPARK	SPRINGS-DALPARK	43 C1
		KRUGERSDORP	GOSFORTH	DALPARK-RAND AIRPORT	43 B1

Key Tourist Areas Legend

National roads Nationalrouten Route nationale	Motorway and interchange Autobahn mit Kreuzungen Autoroute avec échangeur
Motorways Autobahn Autoroute	Game and nature reserves Wild und Naturschutzgebiete Réserves naturelles — *Inyati N.R.*
Principal roads Nationalstraßen Route de liaison régionale	
Main roads Hauptstraßen Route principale — Tar / Untar	Battle sites Ehemaliges Schlachtfeld Lieu de bataille historique — ⚔ *Ulundi*
Minor roads Nebenstraßen Route secondaire — Tar / Untar	Mountain ranges Gebirge Chaîne de montagnes — *LEBOMBO*
Route numbers Routenummern Numéros de routes — N4 R28 R518	Scenic routes Malerische Landschaft Route panoramique
Distances in kilometres Entfernungen in Kilometern Distance en kilomètres — 19 / 15	Mountain passes Bergpässe Cols — *Du Toits*
Railways Eisenbahn Chemin de fer	Border posts Grenzübergang Poste de contrôle — Lebombo
International boundary Internationalgrenze Frontière internationale	Provincial names Provinz Nom du département — **Natal**
Provincial boundary Provinzgrenzen Frontière provinciale	

Airports Flughäfen Aéroports — ✈INT. ✈Other	
Places of interest Sehenswürdigkeiten Endroit à voir — ● *Baobab Tree*	
Stations (selected) Bahnhof (Auswahl) Gare — ●	
Area names Gebiet Nom de la région — Lebowa	
Toll roads Gebührenpfl. Straße Route à péage — ⑦	
Peaks in metres Höhe in Metern Sommet — *Table Mtn.* 1140m ▲	
Water features Gewässer Hydrographie — River / Dam / Swamp	
Major petrol stops Große Tankstelle Station-service — ⛽	

Cities Großstadt Grande ville — ▢	Towns Stadt Ville secondaire — ◉	Large villages Größere Ortschaft Village — ◎	Hotels (selected) Hotel (Auswahl) Hôtel — Ⓗ
Major towns Bedeutende Stadt Ville — ▣	Small towns Kleinstadt Grand village — ○	Villages Dorf Petit village — ○	Camps Ferienlager Camp — ⌂

This bridge crosses the stream where alluvial gold was discovered in 1873, resulting in the settlement at Pilgrim's Rest. Although mining has now ceased, much of the village has been meticulously restored as a living museum.

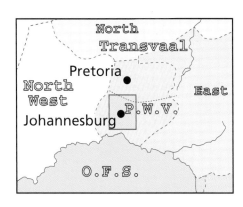

Greater Johannesburg

Vibrant, modern Johannesburg – also called Jo'burg and Egoli – and the independent municipalities that surround the city centre offer a variety of glitzy shopping malls and more informal markets, an impressive range of ethnic and cosmopolitan restaurants, and numerous entertainment venues. To the south, mountainous mine dumps and the rusting headgear of abandoned gold mines are evocative reminders of the days when Johannesburg was essentially a diggers' camp and a tour of Gold Reef City is a must. In the nothern suburbs, many tree-shaded parks and open spaces where indigenous vegetation has been preserved, provide outdoor recreational venues for the city-dwellers.

Gold Reef City, situated on the old Crown Mines site, 6 km (4 miles) south of the central city area, is an evocative reconstruction of pioneer Johannesburg. Visitors here can explore underground workings, watch gold being poured, and enjoy traditional dancing. Other attractions include train and horse-drawn omnibus trips, a Victorian funfair and tea parlour, house museums furnished in period style, and many attractive speciality shops.

For some serious shopping, head north to fashionable and affluent Sandton City; one of the largest, most sophisticated shopping and business complexes in South Africa – indeed, in the southern hemisphere.

Between Sandton City and the city centre are a number of interesting destinations. Just north of the city is The Wilds (Houghton Drive, Houghton) an 18 ha (44-acre) area of rocky ridges, streams and cultivated gardens of indigenous flora which has a network of signposted walking trails.

A little way further north of Houghton is the suburb of Melrose, home of the Melrose Bird Sanctuary which provides a haven for some 120 species of bird.

Directly to the west of Melrose and Houghton is the suburb of Emmarentia which offers a number of attractions. These include: the Johannesburg Botanic Gardens (Thomas Bowler Avenue) which boast a lovely rose garden, fountains, pools and more than 4,000 plants; the Emmarentia Dam, where yachtsmen, boardsailers and model-boat enthusiasts enjoy themselves; and Melville Koppies, a small nature reserve that features indigenous flora, a walking trail and the remains of an Iron-age village and smelting works.

At Blairgowrie, to the north of Emmarentia, is the Florence Bloom Bird Sanctuary. It is a haven to about 200 bird species, many of which congregate around two dams alongside of which hides have been established.

Vintage car enthusiasts should head for the neighbouring suburb of Randburg to visit the Klein Jukskei Motor Museum (Witkoppen Road). It boasts a superb collection of vehicles, including two rare Lincolns and the country's oldest running car, an 1889 Benz.

In the city centre, the MuseumAfrica in Bree Street, the Public Library in Market Street, the Johannesburg Art Gallery in Joubert Park and the Railway Museum in De Villiers Street (the latter includes an excellent art gallery) are among the wide selection of cultural venues offered.

Left: *The communications tower is a well-recognized feature of Johannesburg's skyline; the tallest building, it towers above the concrete-and-glass heart of the city.*
Above: *A family takes a morning stroll through Van Riebeeck Park, one of the 600 public gardens and open spaces that grace Johannesburg and the surrounding suburbs.*

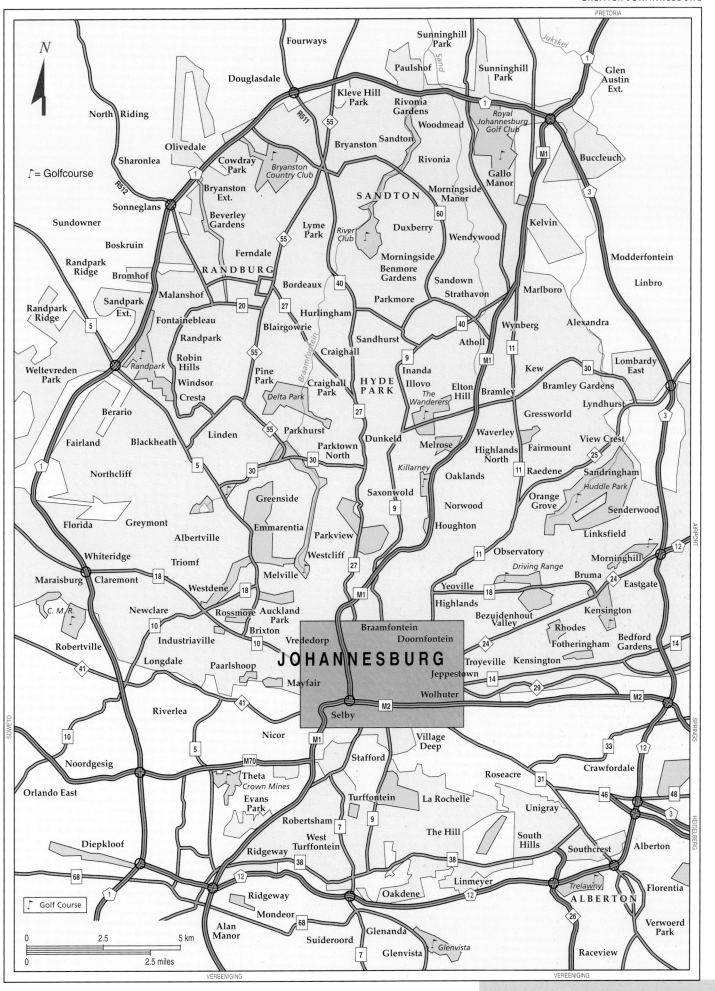

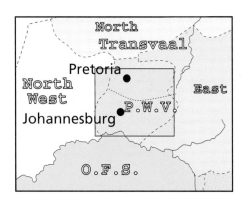

Witwatersrand

Johannesburg and its surrounding areas are known as the Witwatersrand or, more simply, as 'the Rand' or 'the Reef'. The Witwatersrand, in turn, forms a part of what is called the PWV area, which includes Pretoria in the north and the Vaal Triangle to the south, whose 'points' are Vereeniging, Vanderbijlpark and Sasolburg.

A favourite playground of the Witwatersrand's city-dwellers is Hartbeespoort Dam, which lies among the foothills of the Magaliesberg range, 35 km (22 miles) to the west of Pretoria. The waters, 12 km² (5 sq miles) in extent and set in attractive countryside, are a popular haunt of water-sportsmen, angling and boating enthusiasts, and caravanners and campers. Specific attractions in the area are the Aquarium, which features exotic freshwater fish, performing seals and crocodiles; and the Zoo and Snake Park which house a wide variety of reptiles and animals. Snake, chimpanzee and seal 'shows' are held here on Sundays and public holidays.

The dam is not the only attraction within the 120-km (75-mile) long Magaliesberg range. Tourists and locals are enticed here by the tranquillity of the hills and valleys, the lovely scenic drives and gentle walks, the charm of the vistas, and the hospitality of the hotels and lodges. Here, too, the endangered Cape vulture has found a haven.

A group of hikers pauses for a rest on a rocky outcrop in the scenic Magaliesberg range.

JOHANNESBURG	J	F	M	A	M	J	J	A	S	O	N	D
AVERAGE TEMP. °F	68	67	65	60	55	50	51	55	61	63	65	67
AVERAGE TEMP. °C	20	20	18	16	13	10	10	13	16	18	18	19
Hours of Sun Daily	8	8	8	8	9	9	9	10	9	9	8	8
RAINFALL in	5	4	3	2	1	0.5	0.5	0.5	1	3	4	4
RAINFALL mm	131	95	81	55	19	7	6	6	26	72	114	106
Days of Rainfall	15	11	11	9	4	2	1	2	3	10	14	14

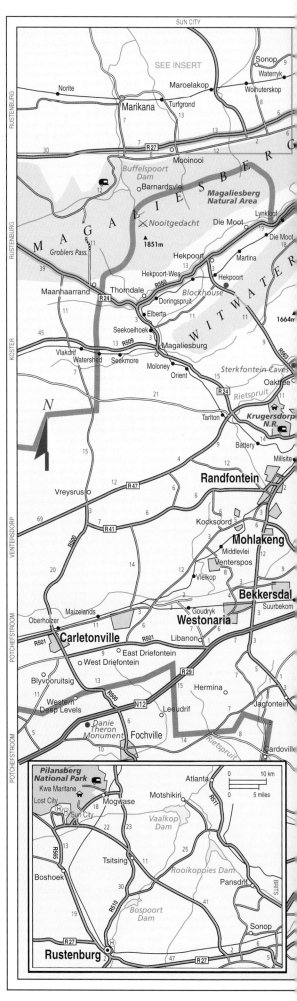

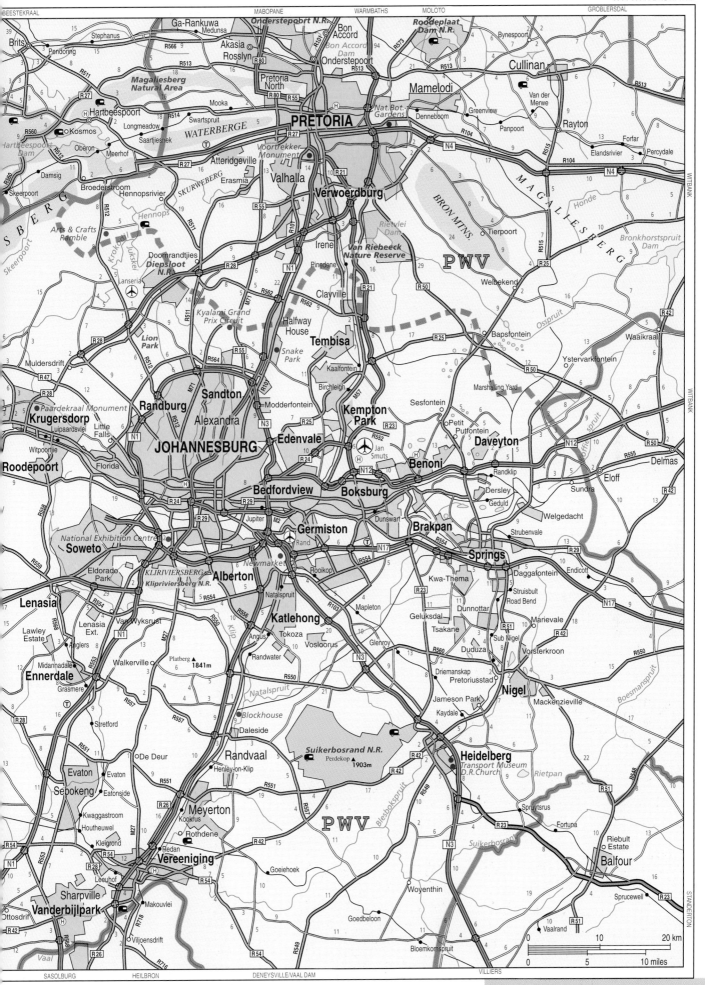

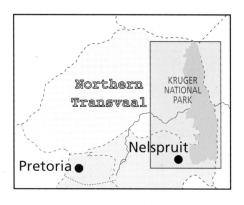

Kruger National Park

South Africa's premier game sanctuary covers nearly 20,000 km² (7,720 sq miles) – an area about the size of Wales and larger than the state of Israel. Because this vast, wild expanse encompasses many different habitats, it is a haven for more varieties of wildlife than any other game reserve in Africa. Among the nearly 140 mammal species found here are the 'big five': lion (of which there are about 1,500); elephant (around 8,000); leopard (around 1,000, although difficult to spot); buffalo (an impressive 25,000); and rhino, of both the black and white varieties. Other large game populations include zebra, wildebeest, giraffe, hippo and crocodile, and there are almost 500 bird species found here.

There are over 20 rest camps scattered throughout the Kruger Park, all pleasantly restful, fenced against the animals and neatly laid out, most of them graced by lovely indigenous trees, flowering plants and expanses of lawn. Accommodation within these camps is generally comfortable and spacious: a typical family cottage has two bedrooms including bedding, a bathroom, toilet, small, fully equipped kitchen, a gauzed-in verandah, air conditioning and a barbecue site outside. Lower down the scale are huts without kitchens, but communal facilities are available.

Camp routine at the Kruger Park is relaxed and undemanding, the emphasis being on low-cost outdoor living. Visitors usually cook their own meals, though all the larger venues have public restaurants. However, for those who really like their comforts, there are some excellent luxury hotels and country hideaways just outside the reserve and within fairly short driving distances of the park's eight entrance gates. Situated on Kruger's west-central boundary are three private game reserves – Timbavati, Manyeleti and Sabie Sand – which boast particularly luxurious game lodge accommodation.

The Kruger Park is open throughout the year, though some low-lying routes may be closed during the summer rains. Altogether there are nearly 2,000 km (1,243 miles) of tarred and gravel roads. Speed limits vary between 40 and 50 km/h (25–30 mph)

In the interests of safety – of both visitors and animals – travel within the park is restricted to daylight hours, and the entrance gates to the park, and the camps, have set opening and closing hours.

For those who want a more intimate experience of the park, a number of informative and undemanding guided wilderness trails are offered.

Many visitors to the Kruger, especially those from overseas, prefer to make their way to the park by air, either on a conducted package tour, or travelling privately. Scheduled Comair flights operate daily between Johannesburg's international airport and the town of Phalaborwa, located just outside the reserve, and Skukuza, the park's headquarters. Car-hire services are available at both of these centres.

NELSPRUIT	J	F	M	A	M	J	J	A	S	O	N	D
AVERAGE TEMP. °F	75	74	73	69	63	59	59	63	66	70	72	73
AVERAGE TEMP. °C	24	24	29	21	18	15	15	7	20	21	22	23
Hours of Sun Daily	7	7	7	8	8	9	9	8	7	6	6
RAINFALL in	5	5	4	2	1	0.5	0.5	0.5	11	2.5	4.5	5
RAINFALL mm	130	119	98	47	19	10	10	10	29	65	114	13
Days of Rainfall	13	12	10	7	4	2	3	3	5	9	13	13

Above: *Accommodation at the various rest camps in the Kruger National Park is generally comfortable and spacious, and consists mostly of rustic, thatched huts. All the major camps have a licensed restaurant, many of which are strategically sited to overlook a waterhole or river.*

Top right : *A lioness lazes in the shade of a tree in the south-central grasslands. The park has a resident population of about 1,500 of these predators.*

Bottom right : *The fish eagle, with its distinctive call, is one of southern Africa's largest and most impressive birds of prey.*

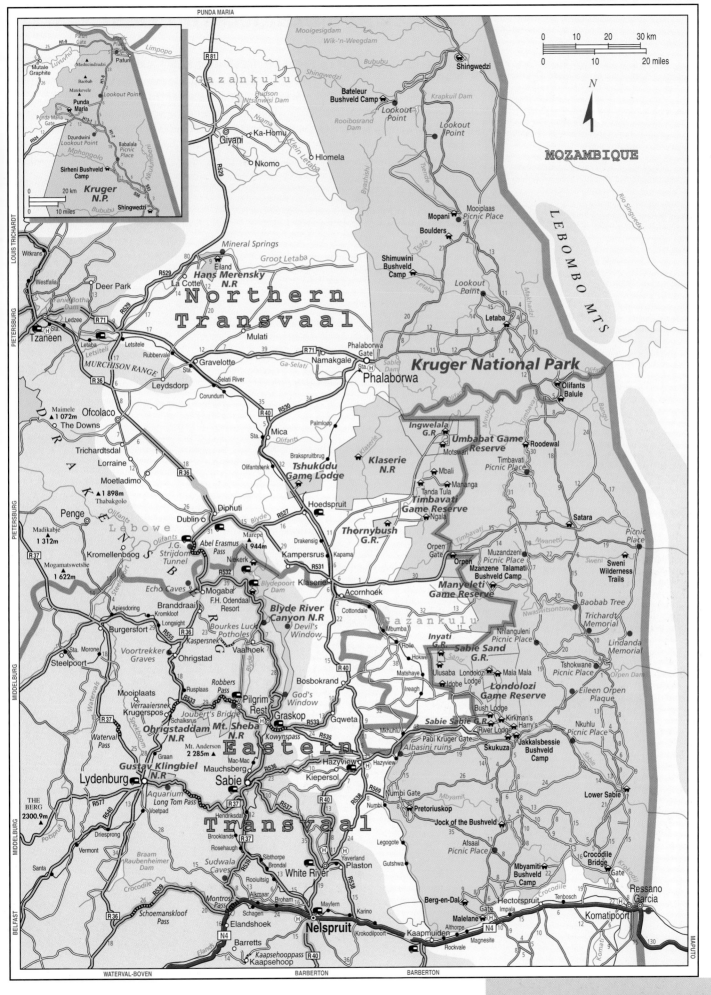

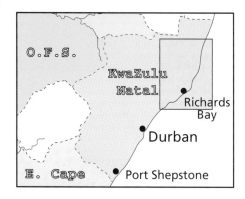

KwaZulu Natal North Coast

Embracing a diversity of natural and cultural assets, KwaZulu Natal's North Coast is a treasure trove for the leisure-seeking visitor. Its long stretches of tropical shoreline, fringed with lush vegetation, are lapped by the warm Indian Ocean. Many of the region's game reserves are rich in wildlife and offer exciting game-viewing. The area's Zulu heritage can be seen in the traditional beehive huts that dot the countryside. Richard's Bay, the region's largest city and industrial hub, centres on its deep-water port, which is the busiest in the country.

Beyond the scenic Dolphin Coast (see page 19), which stretches 100 km (62 miles) north of Durban to the Tugela River mouth, is the region historically known as Zululand.

Inland, where the hills and valleys are luxuriantly green in years with good rains, 'living museums' introduce visitors to aspects of Zulu culture. At Ondini, near Ulundi, Cetshwayo's large royal residence has been reconstructed, and the Nkwaleni Valley between Eshowe and Melmoth is the setting for Shakaland (see page 46).

The conservation areas of KwaZulu Natal support an astonishing variety of animals and birds. Most notable is the Hluhluwe/Umfolozi Park (see page 46) – the oldest of South Africa's many wildlife sanctuaries.

The broad beaches of the North Coast, fringed by lush, tropical growth, attract sunbathers, anglers, divers and boating enthusiasts. Popular venues are the Umlalazi Nature Reserve, St Lucia and Sodwana Bay. Richards Bay, a busy harbour and growing town, has the only officially approved safe bathing beach along this coastline.

Left: A pair of formidable looking black rhino keep a wary eye on the photographer.
Below: A Zulu witchdoctor and his assistant seen standing outside their 'beehive' hut in the Valley of a Thousand Hills.

RICHARDS BAY	J	F	M	A	M	J	J	A	S	O	N	D
AVERAGE TEMP. °F	78	78	77	73	68	63	63	66	69	71	73	77
AVERAGE TEMP. °C	25	25	25	23	20	18	17	19	20	21	23	25
Hours of Sun Daily	7	7	7	8	8	7	8	8	7	6	7	7
SEA TEMP. °F	75	75	75	73	72	70	68	68	68	70	70	73
SEA TEMP. °C	24	24	24	23	22	21	20	20	20	21	21	23
RAINFALL ins.	5.5	5.5	4	4	5	1	2	2	3	4	4	3
RAINFALL mm	144	138	110	111	126	31	47	59	84	97	97	83
Days of Rainfall	12	10	9	9	8	6	8	9	9	10	12	10

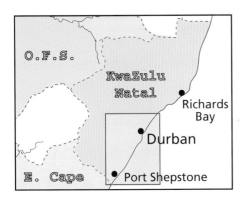

KwaZulu Natal South Coast

A balmy tropical climate, lovely wide expanses of beach, the warm, intensely blue waters of the Indian Ocean, a lushly evergreen hinterland, fine hotels, a score and more of sunlit towns, villages and hamlets, each with its own distinctive personality and its own attractions – these are the ingredients that combine to create one of the southern hemisphere's most enchanting regions. The major city of KwaZulu Natal is Durban, South Africa's third largest metropolis. It has Africa's biggest and busiest harbour and is also one of the country's most popular holiday destinations (see page 60).

Amanzimtoti is a substantial resort town (it has an extensive business district) that offers a wide range of holiday accommodation, restaurants, bars, entertainment, marvellous stretches of sand (the two main beaches are manned by professional life guards all year round), a lagoon and tidal pool (there are boats for hire), and angling from rock and beach.

The nearby Amanzimtoti Bird Sanctuary on Umdoni Road is worth a visit (waterfowl are prominent; the greenbacked herons and peacocks are features; visitor facilities include bird-watching hides, a short walking trail, and teas at weekends). The Ilanda Wilds Nature Reserve is a small but beautiful and richly varied riverine

haven for 160 species of bird and 120 kinds of tree and shrub. There are a number of nature trails and picnic spots.

South of Amanzimtoti the coastline is lined with scores of little towns, villages and hamlets, each with its own distinctive charm and most linked by the excellent N2 coastal highway. Prominent among these is Scottburgh, offering safe bathing, good fishing and Crocworld, which includes a complex of crocodile pens, a wildlife museum, a snake pit and a Zulu village where traditional dances are performed on Sunday afternoons.

Port Shepstone boasts one of the finest golf courses in the country, and lively Margate (the hub of the so-called Hibiscus

Coast) offers beaches and a golf course, hotels and self-catering complexes, shops, restaurants and discos.

Inland from Port Shepstone is the Oribi Gorge Nature Reserve, a magnificent expanse of rugged hills, deep valleys, emerald grassland and a spectacular canyon. For excitement and glamour, the luxurious Wild Coast Sun casino resort further south is only one-and-a-half hours from Durban, and easily accessible from the South Coast Road.

Below: The KwaZulu Natal South Coast is dotted with scores of attractive holiday resorts, such as the little town of Uvongo which is situated at the mouth of the Uvongo River.

Left: The Umzimkulwana River has carved its way through the sandstone to create the magnificent Oribi Gorge. Some 24km long and up to 366m deep, the gorge is protected as a nature reserve and is home to a wealth of animal and bird species.

DURBAN	J	F	M	A	M	J	J	A	S	O	N	D
AVERAGE TEMP. °F	76	76	75	71	66	62	62	63	66	69	72	74
AVERAGE TEMP. °C	24	25	24	22	19	17	16	17	19	20	22	23
Hours of Sun Daily	6	7	7	7	7	7	7	7	6	5	5	6
SEA TEMP. °F	75	77	75	73	70	68	66	66	68	70	72	73
SEA TEMP. °C	24	25	24	23	21	20	19	19	20	21	22	23
RAINFALL in	5	4	5	3	3	1	2	2	3	4	4	4
RAINFALL mm	135	114	124	87	64	26	44	58	65	89	104	108
Days of Rainfall	15	12	12	9	7	5	5	7	10	14	16	15

INDIAN OCEAN

19

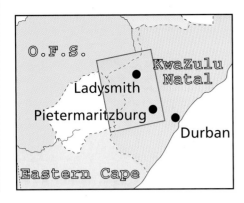

Drakensberg Mountain Resorts

The Drakensberg – South Africa's highest mountain range – is a massive and strikingly beautiful rampart of deep gorges, pinnacles and saw-edged ridges, caves, overhangs and balancing rocks. In the winter months its upper levels lie deep in snow, but clustered among the green foothills far below, in undulating grasslands, is a score of old-established resort hotels that cater well for family holidaymakers. The 'Berg', as this area is fondly called, has much to offer: clean mountain air, numerous hiking paths and horseback trails, precipitous mountain climbs, excellent trout fishing, and some good bowling greens and golf courses.

Two of the most worthwhile holiday destinations in the Drakensberg area are the Royal National Park and the Giant's Castle Game Reserve.

The Royal National Park is an extensive floral and wildlife sanctuary, being home to various antelope and about 200 bird species, among them the black eagle, and the bearded and Cape vultures. There are over 30 recommended walks and hikes ranging from the gentle 3-km (1.8-mile) Otto trail to the 46-km (28-mile) route that takes you to the Mont-aux-Sources plateau, the last stretch involving a chain-ladder ascent up the sheer eastern face.

Particularly recommended is the excursion to the Tugela Falls, where the river plunges into the pools below in a series of cascades; one a sheer drop of 183 m (600 ft), making it the country's highest waterfall.

Numerous bridle paths wind across enchanting landscapes. Horseriding trails are organized at many of the holiday resorts and all rides are accompanied by experienced guides.

Accommodation is available at the Royal National Park Hotel or the elegant Mont-aux-Sources Hotel nearby, as well as at Tendele, the park's luxury lodge. Two rest camps offer bungalows, cottages and camping and caravanning facilities.

Located further south, in central Drakensberg, Giant's Castle, part of the Natal Drakensberg Park, also offers scenic splendour, a comprehensive network of hiking trails, horseback riding, an intriguing plant life (a large number of the Drakensberg's 800 flowering species are found here) and a superb array of birds of prey. During the harsh winter months, to

assist the vultures in obtaining food, they are fed at hides or 'vulture restaurants', thereby affording visitors the opportunity to study and photograph these predatory birds close at hand.

The park is famous for its wealth of Bushman rock art, some of which is on view in the two site museums.

Basic accommodation is available in the Giant's Castle camp or at nearby Injasuti.

ESTCOURT	J	F	M	A	M	J	J	A	S	O	N	D
AVERAGE TEMP. °F	71	71	68	63	56	51	52	55	61	64	67	70
AVERAGE TEMP. °C	21	21	20	17	13	10	11	13	16	18	19	21
Hours of Sun Daily	7	7	7	7	8	8	9	9	8	7	7	7
RAINFALL ins.	6	3.5	2	1.5	0	0	0	1	1	2.5	3.5	5
RAINFALL mm	147	87	74	47	10	6	6	26	37	66	94	129
Days of Rainfall	15	12	12	8	2	2	2	4	6	10	13	14

Left: Natal Midlands' spectacular Howick Falls which plunge 95 m (311 ft) can be seen en route to the Drakensberg.
Above top: Panoramic mountain views, such as this one of the Amphitheatre, are to be found in the Drakensberg's Royal National Park.
Above: The Royal National Park offers hikers a wide variety of walks and trails – some gentle, some arduous.

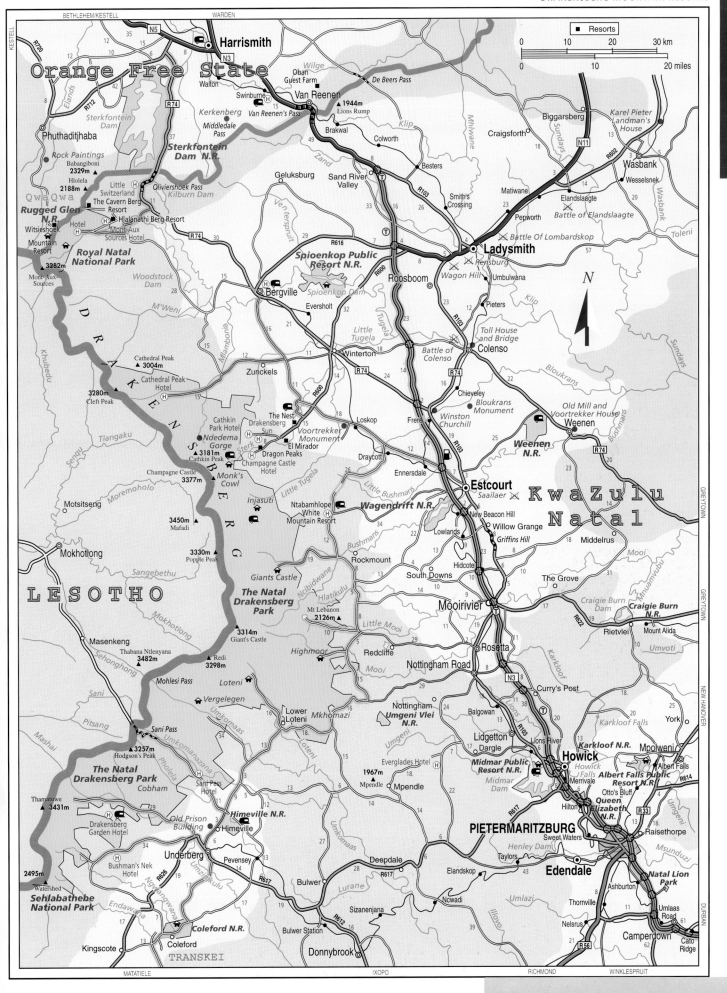

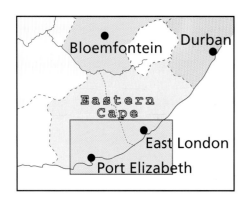

Eastern Cape

This beautiful region of the country has a turbulent history: it was here in the 19th century that white settlers and local inhabitants fought long and bitterly for territorial possession. In fact, many of the area's towns and villages began their lives as garrisoned outposts and fortified settlements. The region retains its wild, natural beauty: inland, there are a number of attractive natural reserves and parks (such as the Addo Elephant National Park, the Zuurberg National Park and the Shamwari Game Reserve), while along the coastline there's an endless succession of superb sandy beaches and excellent fishing venues.

The southern part of the Eastern Cape is rich in tourist attractions. Of particular interest to those with a penchant for beautiful beaches is the strip of coastline between Jeffreys Bay and Cape St Francis. Considered to have the finest surfing waves in the world, this stretch is also renowned for the wealth and variety of its seashells: searching the tideline for these natural

PORT ELIZABETH	J	F	M	A	M	J	J	A	S	O	N	D
AVERAGE TEMP. °F	70	70	69	65	61	58	57	57	60	62	65	68
AVERAGE TEMP. °C	21	21	20	18	16	14	14	14	15	17	18	20
Hours of Sun Daily	9	8	7	7	7	7	7	8	7	8	9	7
SEA TEMP. °F	70	70	68	66	63	61	61	61	63	64	66	70
SEA TEMP. °C	21	21	20	19	17	16	16	16	17	18	19	21
RAINFALL in	2	2	2	2	3	2	2	3	3	2	2	1
RAINFALL mm	41	39	55	57	68	61	54	75	70	59	49	34
Days of Rainfall	2	8	10	9	9	8	8	10	9	11	11	9

treasures is a favourite (and rewarding) pastime among holidaymakers. The area is very well-served with accommodation facilities, which include camping sites, self-contained cottages for hire, and a number of hotels.

Situated 72 km (45 miles) northeast of Port Elizabeth is the Addo Elephant National Park, home to more than 200 elephant. It is also a sanctuary for black rhino, buffalo, eland, kudu and other antelope, and about 170 species of bird. Covered mostly by impenetrable thornbush, it is difficult to locate and observe the wildlife here, but there are game-viewing roads and viewpoints at the waterholes.

Further to the east, half an hour's drive from Port Elizabeth, is the elegant centre of Grahamstown. A focus of academic and cultural life, it is known both as the 'City of Saints' for the number of its churches (40 in all) and as the 'Settler City' for its British colonial origins. Notable cultural venues are the Albany Museum complex and the Observatory Museum.

Grahamstown is famous for its National Festival of the Arts (featuring an exciting variety of drama, music, dance, paintings and sculpture), held here in July every year, to which thousands of people from all over the country flock.

The Addo Elephant National Park offers visitors exciting, close-up views of its once-endangered elephant population.

EAST LONDON	J	F	M	A	M	J	J	A	S	O	N	D
AVERAGE TEMP. °F	71	72	70	67	63	61	60	61	62	64	66	69
AVERAGE TEMP. °C	22	22	21	19	18	16	16	16	17	18	19	21
Hours of Sun Daily	7	7	7	7	7	8	7	7	7	7	7	8
SEA TEMP. °F	66	66	66	64	64	63	63	63	63	64	64	64
SEA TEMP. °C	19	19	19	18	18	17	17	17	17	18	18	18
RAINFALL "	3	4	4	3	2	2	2	3	4	4	4	3
RAINFALL mm	74	95	106	80	55	40	51	75	93	95	90	74
Days of Rainfall	13	12	12	9	9	5	5	7	9	13	12	12

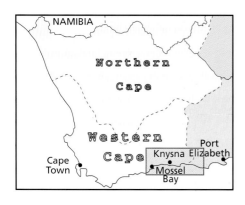

Garden Route

The 220-km (137-mile) Garden Route, stretching from Mossel Bay in the west to Storms River in the east, is one of the most scenically splendid segments of the South African coastline. It is a verdant region of rolling green hills, charming bays and beaches, chains of lakes and thick indigenous forests. The clear blue waters of the ocean are warm in summer, attracting bathers, surfers, sailors, rock anglers and deep-sea fishermen. The region offers many enticements for tourists, being well served with resorts, caravan and camping grounds, attractive marinas and good restaurants.

The most popular attractions along the Garden Route are the picturesque Wilderness Lakes Area, the seaside resorts of Knysna and Plettenberg Bay, and the Tsitsikamma National Park.

The Wilderness Lakes Area is an enchanting stretch of coastline, 28 km (17 miles) in extent, that embraces no less than five rivers and a string of six lakes. Birdlife abounds in the area and bird hides provide the visitor with an opportunity for close-up views of fish eagles, ospreys, herons, kingfishers and many types of waterfowl.

The attractive town of Knysna is situated alongside the Knysna Lagoon, a magnificent stretch of water that opens out to the sea through two imposing cliffs known as The Heads. Cabin cruisers and houseboats are available for hire on the calm waters of this extensive lagoon.

Plettenberg Bay, with its superb beaches, is one of the country's most fashionable resorts. It offers various sports facilities, country inns, discos and boutiques.

The Tsitsikamma National Park, situated further to the east, is richly endowed with plant, animal and bird life. The park is traversed by the popular Otter Walking Trail which leads through 41 km (25 miles) of unsurpassed coastal scenery.

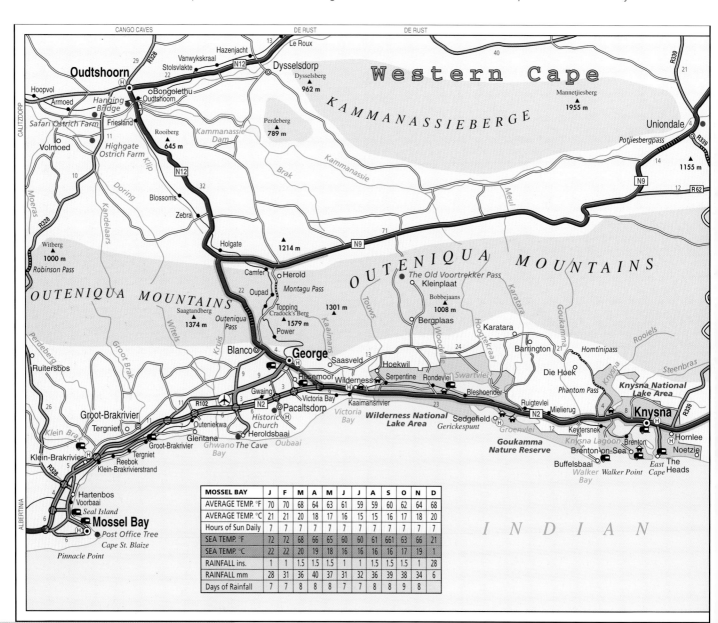

MOSSEL BAY	J	F	M	A	M	J	J	A	S	O	N	D
AVERAGE TEMP. °F	70	70	68	64	63	61	59	59	60	62	64	68
AVERAGE TEMP. °C	21	21	20	18	17	16	15	15	16	17	18	20
Hours of Sun Daily	7	7	7	7	7	7	7	7	7	7	7	7
SEA TEMP. °F	72	72	68	66	65	60	60	61	661	63	66	21
SEA TEMP. °C	22	22	20	19	18	16	16	16	16	17	19	1
RAINFALL ins.	1	1	1.5	1.5	1.5	1	1	1.5	1.5	1.5	1	28
RAINFALL mm	28	31	36	40	37	31	32	36	39	38	34	6
Days of Rainfall	7	7	8	8	8	7	7	8	8	9	8	

Left: *Wilderness, developed around a lagoon at the mouth of the Touws River, is a popular resort town, located some 40 kilometres south of Knysna. It is an excellent venue for a variety of watersports.*

Above: *The impressive Cango Caves, situated close to Oudtshoorn, are one of Africa's most splendid natural wonders.*

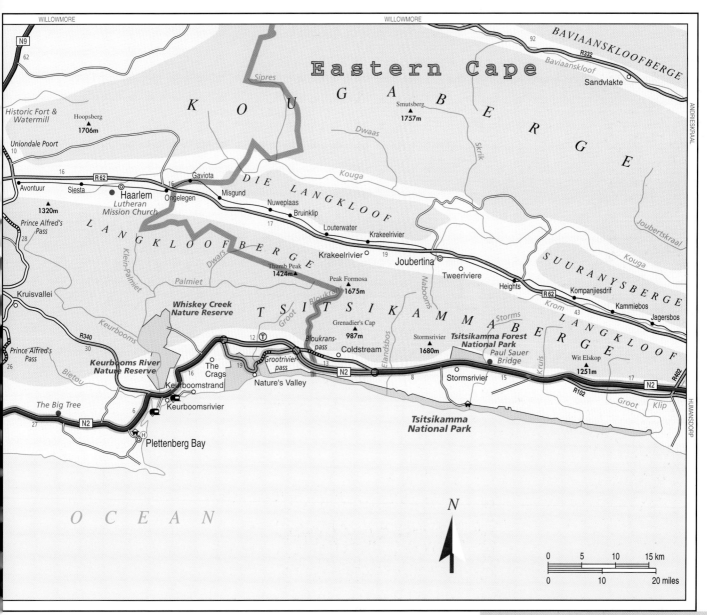

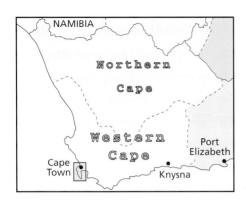

Cape Peninsula

The slender, 75-km (47-mile) long Cape Peninsula comprises, for the most part, a strikingly beautiful pleateau that achieves its loftiest and most spectacular heights in the famed Table Mountain massif that overlooks Table Bay and Cape Town – a neat, bustling little metropolis of handsome buildings, elegant thoroughfares and glittering shops. The western and eastern shorelines of the Peninsula are graced by superb beaches and attractive residential and resort centres that are a magnet for holiday-makers, boating enthusiasts, scuba-divers, surfers and sunworshippers.

The Peninsula's premier attraction is undoubtedly Table Mountain, which soars 1,086 m (3,564 ft) above sea level. You can climb to its summit on foot along one of several charted paths; however, most visitors make the ascent by cable car. The five-minute trip operates all year round, subject to weather conditions.

To the south of Table Mountain are two of the Peninsula's most noteworthy highlights – the Kirstenbosch Botanic Gardens and the Constantia Wine Estates.

Kirstenbosch, situated in the shadow of the Table Mountain range, is among the world's most celebrated botanic gardens with an astonishing array of flowering plants being cultivated here (including thousands of indigenous species). There are delightful walks along the many pathways and the birdlife is enchanting.

The world-famous Groot Constantia, a stately Old Cape Dutch homestead dating from the late 17th century, is notable for its elegant architecture, period furniture, two-storeyed wine cellar, museum and lovely grounds.

The Peninsula's coastline has much to offer in terms of variety. Around the corner from Cape Town is Sea Point, a busy, cosmopolitan seaside suburb. Luxurious apartment buildings line the elegant palm-graced beachfront and the area is well served with restaurants, discos and other nightspots. Close by is Clifton, renowned for its four magnificent beaches, which are favoured by the city's trendier set.

A particularly enchanting spot further down the coast is Hout Bay with its quaint little fishing harbour, from where one can embark on launch trips around the coast.

On the eastern side of the Peninsula, Muizenberg provides some of the area's finest bathing – the water here is much warmer than the western side. Further to the south, Simon's Town – headquarters of the South African Navy – has an old-world charm that is uniquely its own. There are also some excellent beaches close by, notably Seaforth and The Boulders with its protected penguin colony.

Top left: The four beaches of Clifton rank among South Africa's finest.
Bottom left: A seagull's view of part of the Victoria and Alfred Waterfront – one of Cape Town's most successful developments offering fine shops and various excellent restaurants.
Below: Kirstenbosch Gardens has a spectacular variety of indigenous plants, a wealth of birdlife, and a delightful array of scenic walks.

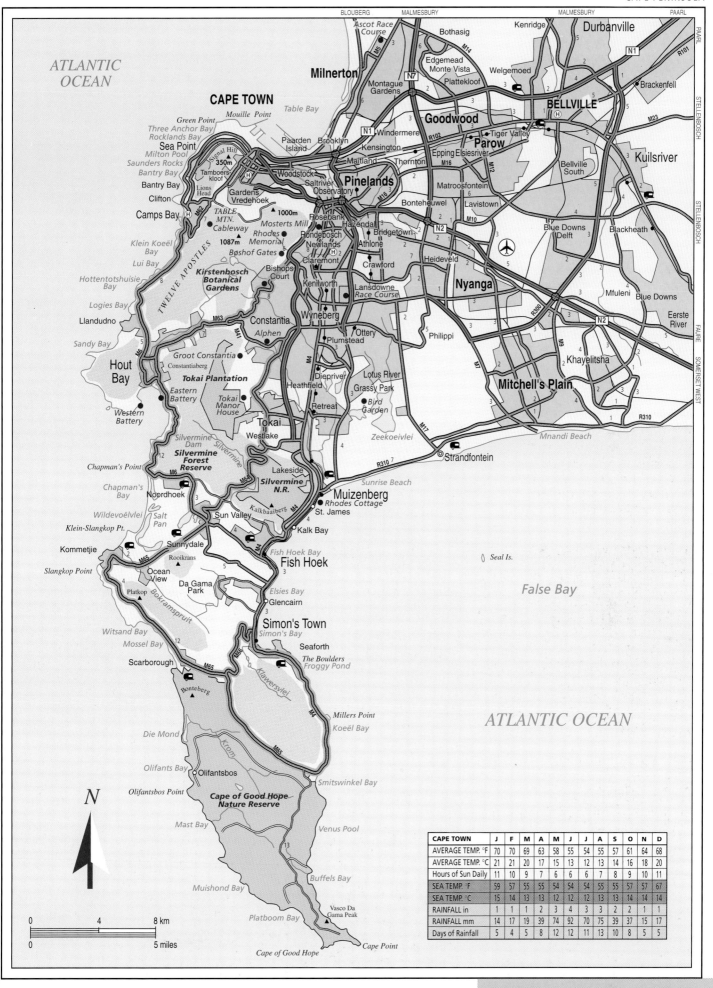

CAPE TOWN	J	F	M	A	M	J	J	A	S	O	N	D
AVERAGE TEMP. °F	70	70	69	63	58	55	54	55	57	61	64	68
AVERAGE TEMP. °C	21	21	20	17	15	13	12	13	14	16	18	20
Hours of Sun Daily	11	10	9	7	6	6	6	7	8	9	10	11
SEA TEMP. °F	59	57	55	55	54	54	54	55	55	57	57	67
SEA TEMP. °C	15	14	13	13	12	12	12	13	13	14	14	14
RAINFALL in	1	1	1	2	3	4	3	3	2	1	1	1
RAINFALL mm	14	17	19	39	74	92	70	75	39	37	15	17
Days of Rainfall	5	4	5	8	12	12	11	13	10	8	5	5

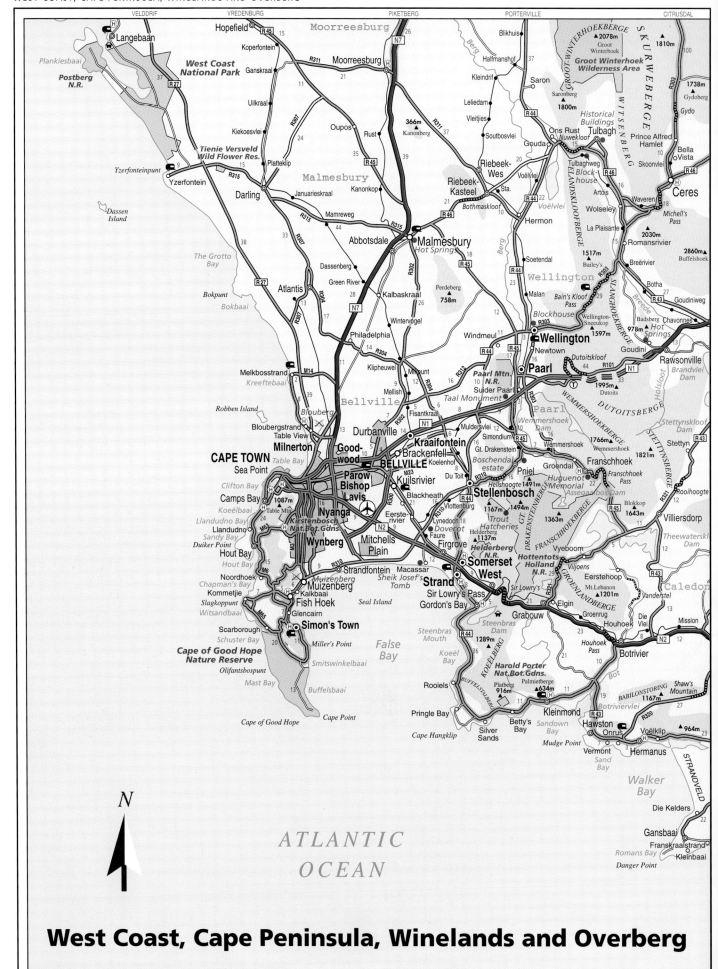

West Coast, Cape Peninsula, Winelands and Overberg

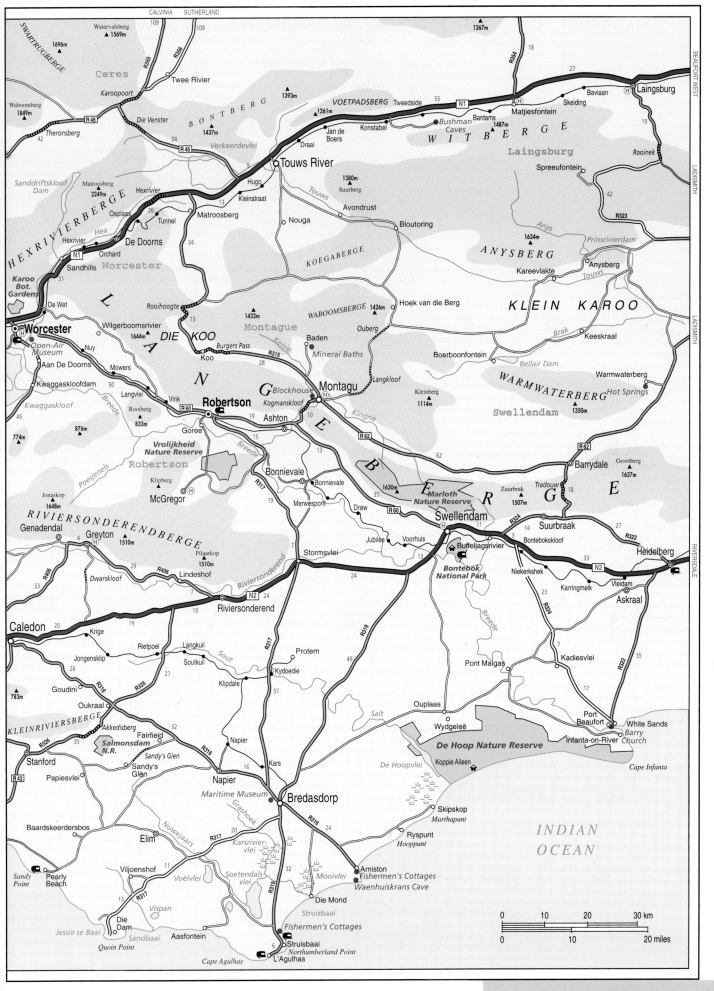

Main Map Section Key and Legend

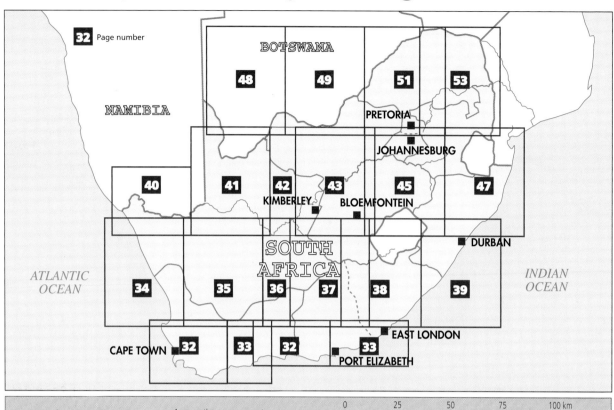

32 Page number

BOTSWANA

NAMIBIA

48   **49**   **51**   **53**

PRETORIA

JOHANNESBURG

40   **41**   **42**   **43**   **45**   **47**

KIMBERLEY   BLOEMFONTEIN

SOUTH AFRICA

DURBAN

ATLANTIC OCEAN

INDIAN OCEAN

34   **35**   **36**   **37**   **38**   **39**

EAST LONDON

CAPE TOWN   **32**   **33**   **32**   **33**

PORT ELIZABETH

Scale 1 : 1,750,000	1 cm on the map represents 1,750,000 cm = 17.5 km actual distance

0   25   50   75   100 km

0   25   50 miles

National roads / Nationalrouten / Route nationale	Motorways and interchanges / Autobahn mit Kreuzungen / Autoroute avec échangeur	Airports / Flughäfen / Aéroports — INT. · Other
Motorways / Autobahn / Autoroute	Game and nature reserves / Wild und Naturschutzgebiete / Réserves naturelles — Inyati N.R.	Places of interest / Sehenswürdigkeiten / Endroit à voir — • Baobab Tree
Principal roads / Nationalstraßen / Route de liaison régionale		
Main roads / Hauptstraßen / Route principale — Tar Untar	Battle sites / Ehemaliges Schlachtfeld / Lieu de bataille historique — ✕ Ulundi	Stations (selected) / Bahnhof (Auswahl) / Gare — •
Minor roads / Nebenstraßen / Route secondaire — Tar Untar		Area names / Gebiet / Nom de la région — Lebowa
Route numbers / Routenummern / Numéros de routes — N4 R28 R518	Mountain ranges / Gebirge / Chaîne de montagnes — LEBOMBO	
Distances in kilometres / Entfernungen in Kilometern / Distance en kilometres — 19 15	Scenic routes / Malerische Landschaft / Route panoramique	Toll roads / Gebührenpfl. Straße / Route à péage — Ⓣ
Railways / Eisenbahn / Chemin de fer	Mountain passes / Bergpässe / Cols — Du Toits	Peaks in metres / Höhe in Metern / Sommet — Table Mtn. ▲1140m
International boundaries / Internationalgrenze / Frontière internationale	Border posts / Grenzübergang / Poste de contrôle — Lebombo	Water features / Gewässer / Hydrographie — River Dam Swamp
Provincial boundaries / Provinzgrenzen / Frontière provinciale	Provincial names / Provinz / Nom du département — Natal	Major petrol stops / Große Tankstelle / Station-service — ⛽

Cities / Großstadt / Grande ville — ☐	Towns / Stadt / Ville secondaire — ⊙	Large villages / Größere Ortschaft / Village — ◎	Hotels (selected) / Hotel (Auswahl) / Hôtel — Ⓗ
Major towns / Bedeutende Stadt / Ville — ◩	Small towns / Kleinstadt / Grand village — ○	Villages / Dorf / Petit village — ∘	Camps / Ferienlager / Camp — ⌂

Eastern and Western Cape

Dominated by series after series of soaring mountain ranges, interspersed with rolling wheatfields, fruit orchards and vineyards, the southern part of the country is unquestionably one of the most beautiful areas of South Africa. Inland there are forests, deep, fertile valleys, and spectacular mountain passes to explore, while its rugged, rocky coastline offers the visitor countless venues for bathing, surfing, beachcombing and fishing, and a number of delightful holiday villages and towns.

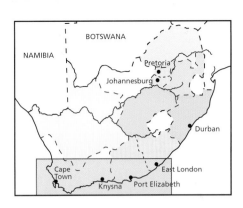

One of the great attractions of the Western Cape are the scores of wineland towns situated in the rich countryside to the east of Cape Town. These include gracious Stellenbosch, which boasts some of the finest Old Cape Dutch architecture in the country, and Franschhoek which still retains much of the French influence of its early Huguenot founders. Tourists can explore the winelands and visit the many estates on various official wine routes that have been established.

The southern coastline of South Africa has much to offer, and two particularly recommended day drives from Cape Town are to the pleasant cliffside town of Hermanus, from where scores of southern right whales can be seen cavorting close off the shore during the mid-winter months; and to the Langebaan Lagoon, situated on the West Coast, with its wealth of birdlife that includes tens of thousands of waders. Both places are popular getaway spots for Capetonians and visitors.

Further to the east, from the holiday town of Mossel Bay onwards, is the famous Garden Route (see page 24), and the southern region of the Eastern Cape that stretches from Port Elizabeth to East London (see page 22).

Fish Hoek is one of the many superb, safe beaches, set against a backdrop of soaring mountain peaks, that are perhaps the Cape Peninsula's biggest drawcard.

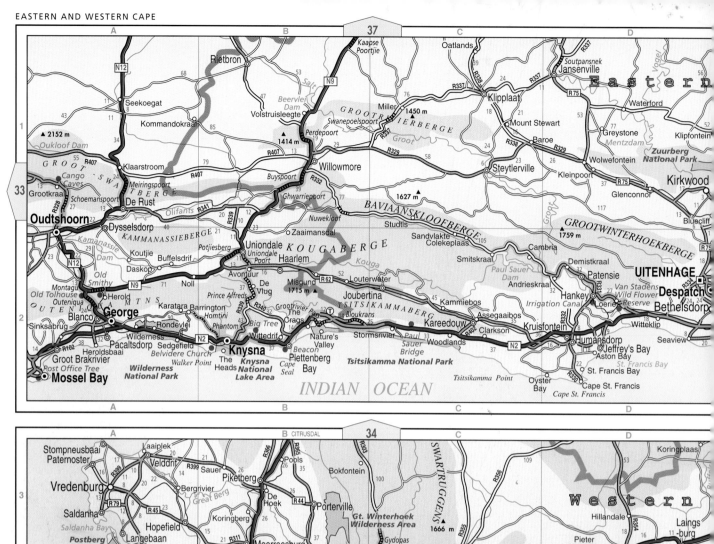

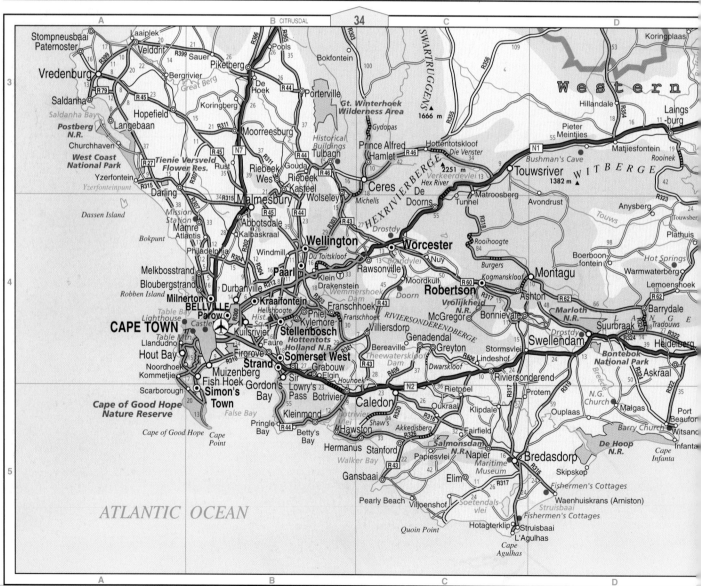

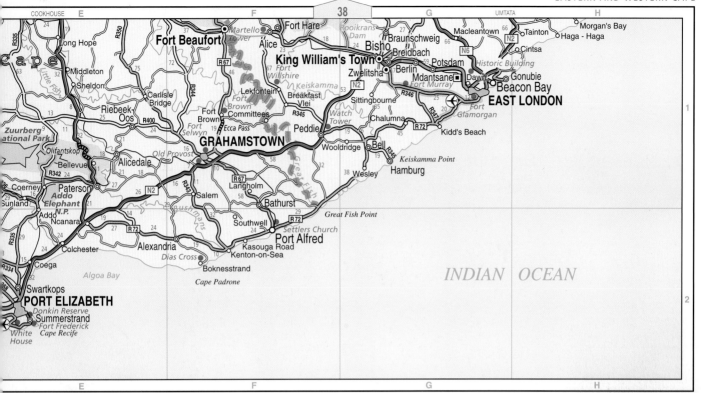

COOKHOUSE · E · 24 · F · 38 · G · UMTATA · H
Long Hope · Fort Beaufort · Martello Tower · Fort Hare · Rooikrans Dam · Braunschweig · Macleantown · Tainton · Morgan's Bay · Haga - Haga
Middleton · Alice · King William's Town · Bisho · Breidbach · Potsdam · N6 · Cintsa
Sheldon · Carlisle Bridge · Fort Willshire · Zwelitsha · Berlin · Mdantsane · Dawn · Gonubie · Beacon Bay
Riebeek Oos · Lekfontein · Breakfast Vlei · Sittingbourne · N2 · Fort Murray · Historic Building · EAST LONDON
Zuurberg National Park · Fort Brown · Committees · Peddie · Watch Tower · Chalumna · Fort Glamorgan
Olifantskop · GRAHAMSTOWN · Old Provost · Wooldridge · Bell · Kidd's Beach
Bellevue · Alicedale · Keiskamma Point
Coerney · Paterson · Salem · Langholm · Wesley · Hamburg
Addo Elephant N.P. · Bathurst
Addo · Ncanara · Southwell · Great Fish Point
Colchester · Alexandria · Port Alfred · Settlers Church
Coega · Kasouga Road · Kenton-on-Sea
Swartkops · Dias Cross · Boknesstrand · INDIAN OCEAN
PORT ELIZABETH · Algoa Bay · Cape Padrone
Donkin Reserve · Summerstrand
Fort Frederick · Cape Recife
White House

BEAUFORT WEST · E · F
Kruidfontein
Zwarts
Prince Albert Road · Dwyka
Cape · N1 · Koup
Vleifontein · Gamkapoort Dam · Prince Albert · 2152 m
Oukloof Dam · Swartberg Pass
Vlieland · Bosluiskloof · GROOT-SWART BERGE
Seweweekspoort · Matjiesrivier
Seweweekspoort Pass · Kruisrivier
Kraaldorings
KLEIN SWARTBERGE · Huisrivier Pass
Ladismith · Zoar · R62 · De Hoop
Calitzdorp · 32
Rooiberg · Oosdam
Rooibergpas
Groot · Van Wyksdorp
Klein-Karoo · Robinson · Cloetes Pass
Tollhouse · OUTENIQUA MTNS.
andrivier · Ruitersbos
Garcias · Langberg
BERGE · Herbertsdale · KNYSNA
Riversdale · Du Plessis · Brandwag
N2
Vermaaklikheid · Albertinia · Mossel Bay
Vleesbaai
Still Bay East · Vleesbaai · Kanonpunt · Gouritsmond
Sebastian Bay · Still Bay West · Groot-Jongensfontein
Cape Barracouta

Above: *The dramatic sandstone crags of the Hex River range rise to some 2,000 m (6,600 ft) above sea level. In the beautiful, fertile valley below, land is intensely cultivated and about 200 farms in the area produce many of the country's export-quality table grapes.*

Left: *Built in 1910, Welgeluk is one of the most splendid examples of the 'feather palaces' that still exist today. This gracious homestead, now a national monument, is part of the Safari Ostrich Show Farm which is open to the public and offers guided tours.*

40

VIOOLSDRIF

A | B | C | D

Dabenoris

Lekkersing

Brak

Cliff Point

Aggeneys

Aninaus Pass

Port Nolloth

Steinkopf

74

R382

93

N7

R64

109

McDougall's Bay

44

Wedge Point

Nigramoep

Bulletrap

Concordia

10

R355

93

Nababeep

13

Okiep

Goegap N.R.

Grootmis

Buffels

Springbok

Miners' Memorial

Van der Stel's
Copper Mine 1685

Kleinsee

Uitkyk

Kommaggas

Mesklip

72

R355

Melkbospunt

Burke's Pass

Gamoep

Messelpad

Wildeperdehoek

68

Scenic Route:
Wild flowers in
Spring (Aug. - Sept.)

Skulpfonteinpunt

Soebatsfontein

43

Stofvlei

Kamieskroon

Kamiesberg

Platbakkies

Koiingnaas

46

Witwater

34

Hondeklipbaai

Karkams

Spoegrivier

Aalwynsfontein

Wallekraal

Strandfonteinpunt

Garies

Swart-Doring

Kliprand

1024 m

Groen

Nariep

58

69

875 m

Groenriviersmond

R358

Island Point

Rietpoort

Kotzesrus

Bitterfontein

16

Nuwerus

Sout

Komkans

R363

60

70

Landplaas

ATLANTIC

Scenic Route:
Wild flowers in
Spring (Aug. - Sept.)

Olifants

Lutzville

24

Vanrhynsdorp

R362

27

24

OCEAN

Papendorp

Vredendal

R27

3

R27

R362

22

N7

Strandfontein

15

Klawer

Olifan
Irrigati

21

R363

Doringbaai

55

Fishing is the principal occupation of the residents here at
Lambert's Bay, one of the small coastal ports found along the
west coast of the country.

Rooiduinepunt

Heerenlogement
Cave

Heerenlogement

53

Ratelfontein

Lambert's Bay

29

16

Graafwa

R364

11

19

Leipoldtville

R365

13

Sandber

29

Elandsbaai

Baboon Point

29

R27

24

R366

27

Redelinghuys

Paleisheu

Noordkuil

18

Het Kruis

St. Helena Bay

Stompneuspunt

Dwarskersbos

48

Stompneusbaai

St.
Helena
Bay

Aurora

Velddrif

20

PIKETBERG

17

21

LAMBERT'S BAY	J	F	M	A	M	J	J	A	S	O	N	D
AVERAGE TEMP. °F	63	63	63	61	59	57	55	55	57	59	61	63
AVERAGE TEMP. °C	17	17	17	16	15	14	13	13	14	15	16	17
Hours of Sun Daily	7	6	7	7	8	8	8	7	6	7	7	7
RAINFALL in	0	0	0	0.5	1	1	1	1	0.5	0	0	0
RAINFALL mm	3	2	6	15	20	21	22	18	11	8	4	5
Days of Rainfall	1	1	1	3	5	5	5	5	3	2	1	1

A | B | C | D

32

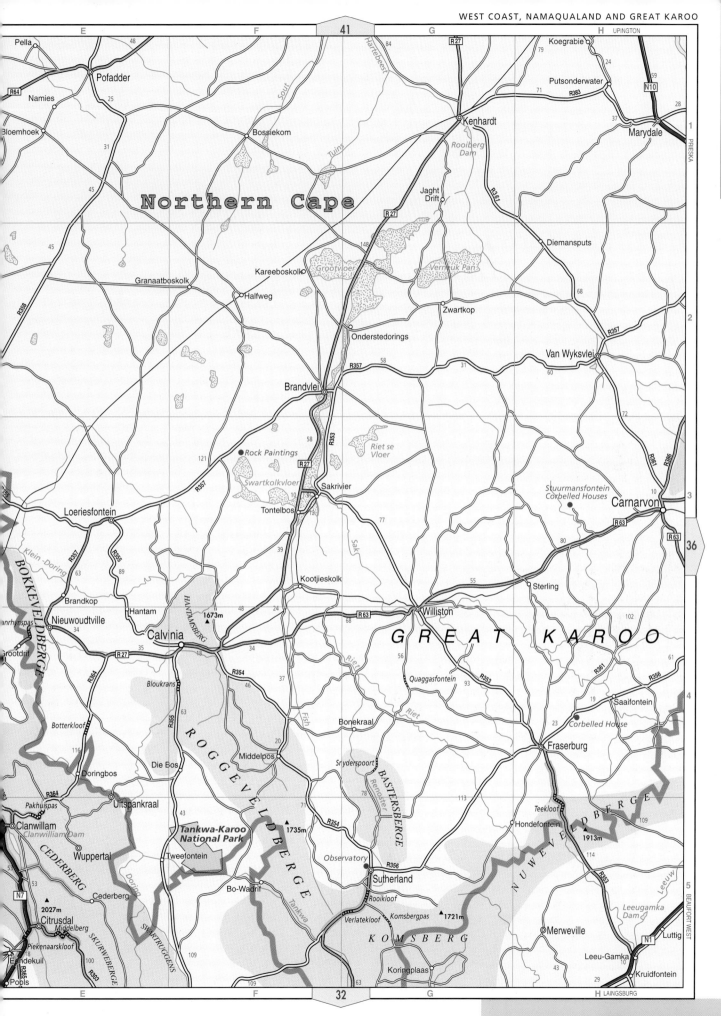

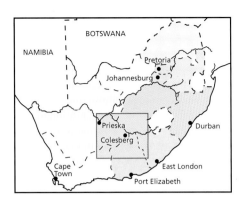

The Great Karoo

The Great Karoo dominates the central Cape interior; it's a semi-arid region of bone-dry air, intense sunshine, minimal rainfall and a haunting beauty of its own. The landscape consists for the most part of far horizons, lonely farmsteads, and endless flocks of sheep. The roads through this area are generally good and straight.

The most notable towns in this region of wide open spaces are Beaufort West and Graaff-Reinet.

Beaufort West is noted for its pleasant pear-tree-lined streets, and as the birthplace of the famed heart surgeon Chris Barnard, many of whose awards are on display in the local museum. Situated just to the north of the town is the Karoo National Park; reintroduced game to be seen here includes Cape mountain zebra and a variety of antelope.

About 200 km (124 miles) to the east of Beaufort West is the town of Graaff-Reinet – a neat, well-ordered place with some fine old architecture and the third oldest town in the Cape. A remarkable natural wonder situated close by is the Valley of Desolation – a fantasia of wind-eroded and strangely shaped dolerite peaks, pillars and balancing rocks that loom over the town.

Well worth a visit is the hamlet of Nieu Bethesda, 50 km (31 miles) to the north, whose principal attraction is the Owl House. Once a private home, now a museum, the Owl House is filled with bizarre and fascinating sculptures created by its late owner, Helen Martins.

A spectacular array of weird rock formations greet visitors at the Valley of Desolation, a natural wonder situated close to the Karoo town of Graaff-Reinet.

COLESBERG	J	F	M	A	M	J	J	A	S	O	N	D
AVERAGE TEMP. °F	77	73	70	61	55	48	50	54	61	64	70	73
AVERAGE TEMP. °C	25	23	21	16	13	9	10	12	16	18	21	23
Hours of Sun Daily	7	6	7	7	8	8	8	7	6	7	7	7
RAINFALL ins.	1	2.5	2.5	1.5	1	0	0	0	1	1	1.5	1.5
RAINFALL mm	47	63	65	39	23	11	10	12	18	29	37	39
Days of Rainfall	5	6	6	5	3	2	1	2	3	4	4

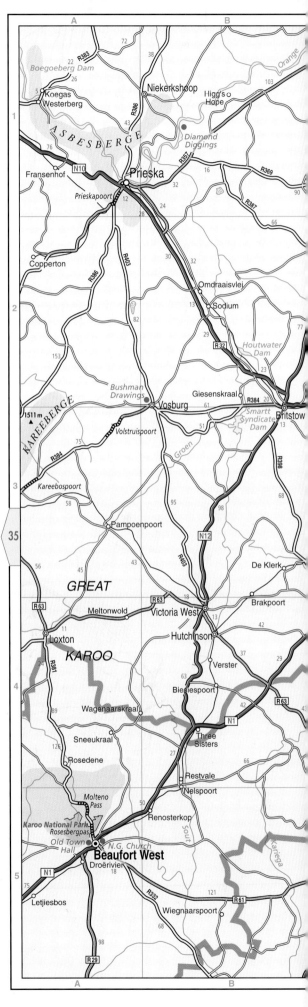

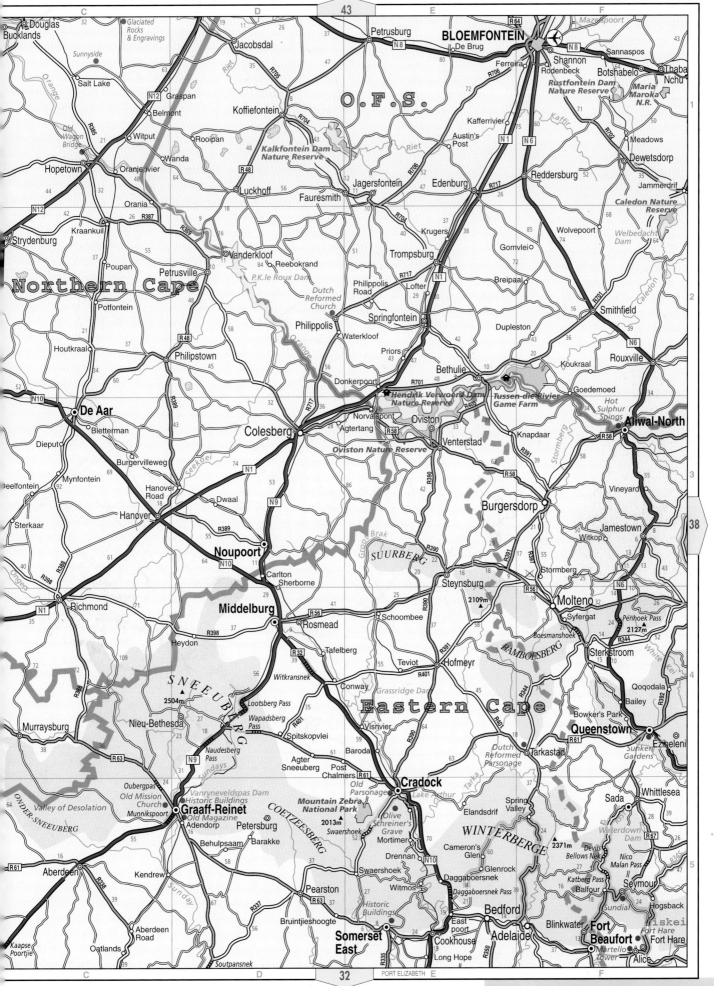

43

LESOTHO

MALUTI

CENTRAL RANGE

DRAKENSBERG

THABA PUTSOA

O.F.S.

Transkei

Eastern Cape

Ciskei

Wild Coast

BLOEM-FONTEIN

MASERU

Ladybrand

Aliwal North

Burgersdorp

Queenstown

UMTATA

Fort Beaufort

Adelaide

Mokhotlong

Kroonstad

Mazelspoort
Sannaspos
Shannon
Rodenbeck
Ferreira
Botshabelo
Thaba Nchu
Tweespruit
Westminster
Pekabrug
Peka
Kolonyama
Mamates
Corn Exchange
Matlameng
Pitseng
Koenong
Kao
Letseng-La-Terae
Mothae

Rustfontein Dam Nature Reserve
Maria Maroka N.R.
Leurivier Dam
Glenrock
Kommissiepoort
Teyateyaneng
Mateka
Sefikeng
Moletsane
St. Martin
Tlokoeng
Motsitseng

Kafferrivier
Meadows
Hobhouse
Mazenod Institute
Roma
Makhaleng
Marakabei
Mantsonyane
Thaba Tseka
Linakeng

Dewetsdorp
Wepener
Van Rooyen's Gate
Morija
Tlali
Ramabanta
Katse Dam
Highlands Water Scheme

Reddersburg
Jammerdrif
Mafeteng
Malealea
Ralegheka
Nkau
Qabane
Sehonghong
The Natal Drakensberg Park

Edenburg
Wolveport
Caledon Nature Reserve
Welbedacht Dam
Thabana Morena
Sepapus Gate
Mpharane
Qobong
Nohana
Mokopung
Patlong
Matsaile

Gomvleio
Vanstadensrus
Boesmanskop
Egmont Dam
Cannibal Caves
Makhaleng Bridge
Mohales Hoek
Kubung
Chief Moorosi's Fortress
Sehlabathebe National Park

Breipaal
Dupleston
Smithfield
Zastron
Mekaling
Phamong
Mt. Moorosi
Paul Kruger Inscription
Mphaki
Lehlohonolo

Bethulie
Koukraal
Rouxville
Goedemoed
Sterkspruit
Palmietfontein
Telebrug
Moyeni
Sebapala
Tosing
Ralebona
Thaba Chitja
Ongeluksnek
Roamer's Rest
Matatiele
New Amalfi

Knapdaar
Hot Sulphur Springs
Herschel
Bluegums
Rock Paintings
Kinirapoort
Sigoga
Cedarville

Vineyard
Lady Grey
Karringmelkspruit
New England
Lundin's Nek
Mosesh's Ford
Naudesnek
Elands Height
Lower Pitseng
Lahlangubo
Moordenaarsnek
Colonanek
Rode

Jamestown
Witkop
Clanville
Clifford
Barkly East
Mount Fletcher
Halcyon Drift
Triple Streams
Mount Frere

Stormberg
Swempoort
Rossouw
Barkly Pass
Maclear
Ugie
Ntywenke
Tyira
Tina Bridge
Qumbu

Molteno
Syfergat
Boesmanshoek
Dordrecht
Morristown
Cala Road
Elliot
Ku-Mayima
Tsolo
Tsitsa Bridge
Sidwadweni
Stoneyridge

Indwe
Garryowen
Calapas
Qiba
Cala
Whitmore
Ntibane
Coghlan
Nobantu
Libode
Misty Mount
Ngqeleni
Old Bunting

Sterkstroom
Braunville
Lady Frere
Askeaton
Lufuta
Engcobo
Langdon
All Saints Nek
Clarkebury
Bashee Bridge
Viedgesville
Mqanduli
Notintsila

Qoqodala
Bailey
Bowker's Park
eZibeleni
Southeyville
Ncora
Nobokwe
Munyu
Bityi
Ngqungu
Elliotdale

Tarkastad
Sunken Gardens
Bolotwa
Qamata
Tsomo
Ntseshe
Cofimvaba
St Marks
Xolobe
Nqamakwe
Idutywa
Ebende
Old Morley
Tshani
Coffee Bay

Elandsdrif
Spring Valley
Sada
Whittlesea
Waqu
Swart Kei
Nobokwe
Taleni
Willowvale
Nyokana
Alderley
Rothmere
Mnewasa Point

Cameron's Glen
Glenrock
Tylden
Cathcart
Bolo Reserve
Qoboqobo
Ciko
Hobeni

Balfour
Seymour
Hogsback
Stutterheim
Bethel
Mgwali
Kei Cuttings
Great Kei River Bridge
Komga
Manubi
Qora Mouth
Mazeppa Bay
The Haven
Dwesa Nature Reserve

Bedford
Blinkwater
Fort Hare
Alice
Kei Road
Amabele
Mpetu
Macleantown
Tainton
Quko
Kei Mouth
Morgan's Bay
Qolora Mouth
Haga-Haga
Wavecrest
Nqabara

Winterberg
Bamboesberg
Stormberg

King Williams Town
EAST LONDON

33

HARRISMITH · MTUBATUBA

INDIAN OCEAN

Cathedral Peak · Cathkin Park · Champagne Castle · White Mountain · Drakensberg Sun · The Natal Drakensberg Park · LESOTHO · ▲ 3482 m · Sani Pass · Drakensberg Garden · Himeville N.R. · Coleford N.R. · Underberg · Himeville · Bulwer · Franklin · Eastern Cape · Swartberg · Sneezewood · Kingscote · Riverside · Creighton · Donnybrook · Bush Reserve · Bonny Ridge · Mount Currie N.R. · Stafford's Post · Kokstad · Brooks Nek · Fort Donald · Mtsizwa · Mount Ayliff · Taban Lukulu · Ngabeni · Magusheni · Bizana · Flagstaff · Holy Cross · Palmerton · Lusikisiki · Umtentu · Gemvale · Embotyi · Utshilini · Mombo · Port St. Johns · Mt Thesiger N.R.

Frere · Loskop · Estcourt · Weenen · Keate's Drift · The Ranch · Bloukrans Monument · Muden · Greytown · Mooirivier · Redcliffe · Rosetta · Nottingham Road · Lidgetton · Dargle · Howick · Albert Falls N.R. · Falls Queen · Midmar Dam N.R. · Hilton · Mpendle · Edendale · PIETERMARITZBURG · Natal Lion Park · Church Elizabeth Park · Thornville · Camperdown · Kranskloof N.R. · Mpumalanga · Hammarsdale · Richmond · Rosebank · Nshongweni Dam · Stainbank N.R. · Ixopo · uMzimkhulu · Umzimkulu Bridge · Highflats · Vernon Crookes N.R. · Bisi · Braemar · St. Faiths · Kwa Dweshula · Harding · Bontrand · Weza · Oribi Gorge N.R. · Marburg · Ngabeni · Paddock · Izingolweni · Izotsha · Port Shepstone · Shelley Beach · Uvongo · Margate · Ramsgate · Southport · Sea Park · Umzumbe · Hibberdene · Turton · Mtwalume · Ifafa Beach · Sezela · Pennington · Kelso · Park Rynie · Scottburgh · Clansthal · uMzinto · Umkomaas · Umgababa · Kingsburgh · Amanzimtoti · Umbogintwini · Isipingo · Umlazi · Adams Mission · Umbumbulu · Queensburgh · Pinetown · Clermont · KwaMashu · DURBAN · The Bluff · Stainbank N.R. · Redoubt · Munster · Southbroom · Palm Beach · Glenmore Beach · Banner Rest · Port Edward · Umtamvuna N.R. · Impisi · Mkambati N.R. · South Sand Bluff · Port Grosvenor

Greytown · Ahrens · Kranskop · Fort Mtombeni · Fort Mombeni · Sevenoaks · New Hanover · Dalton · Mpolweni · Mapumulo · Ndwedwe · Valley of 1000 Hills · Nagledam N.R. · Shakaskraal · Tongaat · Verulam · Inanda · Camperdown

Cetshwayo's Grave · Site of Shaka's Kraal · Empangeni · Entumeni · Coward's Bush Monument · Hinza Forest Reserve · Eshowe · Nonggai Fort · Fort Kwa-Mondi · Amatikulu · Gingindlovu · Mandini · Tugela · Darnall · Tugela Mouth · Fort Pearson · Ultimatum Tree · Stanger · Groutville · Shaka's Memorial · Blythdale Beach · Sheffield Beach · Salt Rock · Shaka's Rock · Ballito · Newsel & Umdloti Beach · Umhlanga Rocks · Richards Bay · Felixton · Richards Bay Nature Reserve · Umlalazi Nature Reserve · Mtunzini · Mzingazi Lake

KwaZulu Natal · Eastern Cape · Transkei · Coast

Ornately decorated rickshaws, drawn by Zulus in lavish, beaded outfits, are one of the most colourful features of Durban's popular beachfront.

DURBAN	J	F	M	A	M	J	J	A	S	O	N	D
AVERAGE TEMP. °F	76	76	75	71	66	62	62	63	66	69	72	74
AVERAGE TEMP. °C	24	25	24	22	19	17	16	17	19	20	22	23
Hours of Sun Daily	6	7	7	7	7	7	7	7	6	5	5	6
SEA TEMP. °F	75	77	75	73	70	68	66	66	68	70	72	73
SEA TEMP. °C	24	25	24	23	21	20	19	19	20	21	22	23
RAINFALL in	5	4	5	3	3	1	2	2	3	4	4	4
RAINFALL mm	135	114	124	87	64	26	44	58	65	89	104	108
Days of Rainfall	15	12	12	9	7	5	5	7	10	14	16	15

Northern Cape

Left: One of the most impressive sights to be found in the Northern Cape is the Augrabies Falls where the Orange River plunges through a massive canyon (up to 250 m/820 ft deep) in a dramatic sequence of rapids and cascades. The surrounding countryside is a desolate land of scrub, sand and rock.

Far left: The Northern Cape town of Upington boasts the longest palm-lined avenue in the world – 1.4 km (0.87 miles) in length. The town is a convenient stopover for visitors on their way to the Augrabies Falls National Park or Kalahari Gemsbok National Park.

UPINGTON	J	F	M	A	M	J	J	A	S	O	N	D
AVERAGE TEMP. °F	81	80	76	68	60	55	54	56	64	70	76	80
AVERAGE TEMP. °C	28	27	25	20	16	12	12	14	18	21	24	26
Hours of Sun Daily	11	11	10	10	9	9	9	10	10	11	11	12
RAINFALL in	2	1.5	1.5	1	0.5	0	0	0	0	0	0.5	1
RAINFALL mm	28	39	37	23	12	4	2	4	3	10	15	18
Days of Rainfall	4	6	6	4	3	2	1	1	1	2	3	3

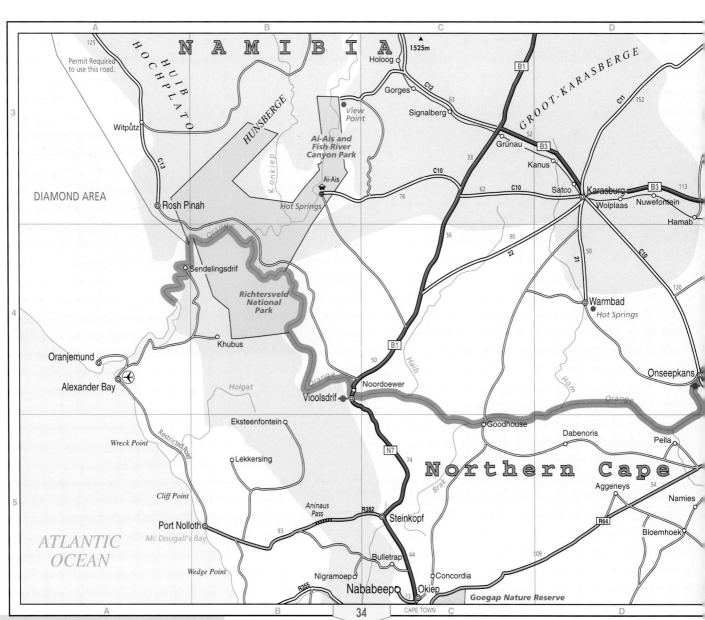

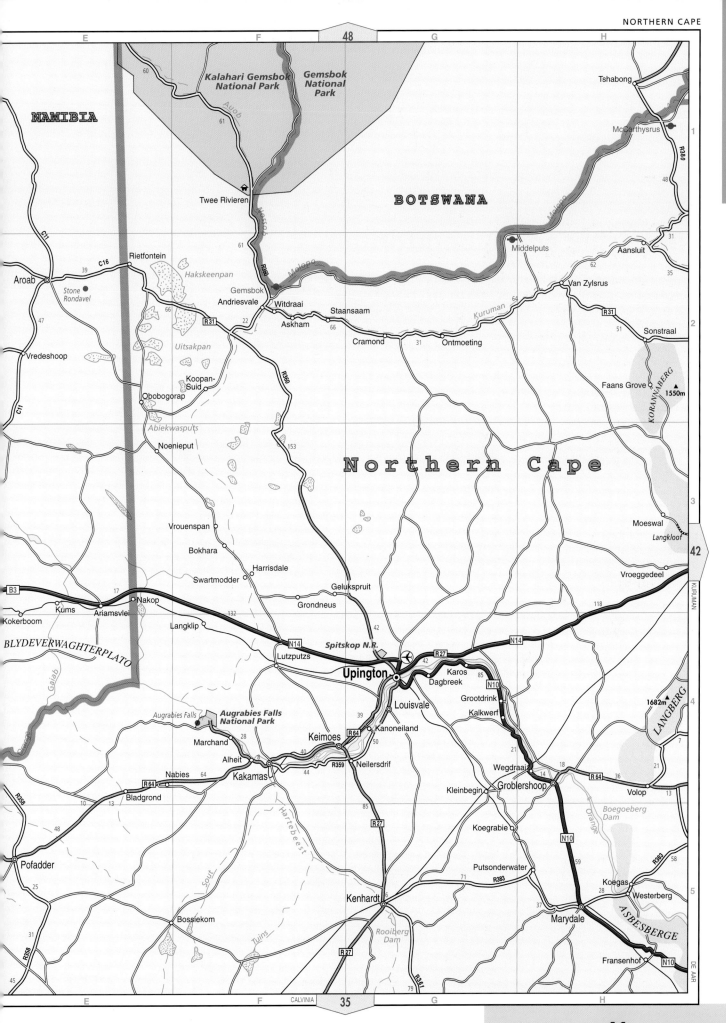

NAMIBIA

Kalahari Gemsbok National Park

Gemsbok National Park

BOTSWANA

Tshabong

McCarthysrus

Twee Rivieren

Middelputs

Aansluit

Van Zylsrus

Rietfontein

Hakskeenpan

Gemsbok

Sonstraal

Andriesvale

Witdraai

Staansaam

Askham

Cramond

Ontmoeting

Uitsakpan

Koopan-Suid

Faans Grove

1550m

Obobogorap

Abiekwasputs

Noenieput

Northern Cape

Moeswal

Langkloof

Vrouenspan

Bokhara

Vroeggedeel

Harrisdale

Swartmodder

Gelukspruit

Grondneus

Langklip

Spitskop N.R.

Lutzputs

Karos

Dagbreek

Upington

Grootdrink

Louisvale

Kalkwerf

Augrabies Falls

Augrabies Falls National Park

Kanoneiland

Keimoes

Marchand

Alheit

Neilersdrif

Wegdraai

Nabies

Kakamas

Kleinbegin

Groblershoop

Volop

Bladgrond

Koegrabie

Pofadder

Putsonderwater

Koegas

Westerberg

Bossiekom

Kenhardt

Marydale

Fransenhof

Aroab

Stone Rondavel

Vredeshoop

Kums

Nakop

Kokerboom

Ariamsvlei

BLYDEVERWAGHTERPLATO

Gaiab

Orange

Hartebeest

Sout

Tuins

Rooiberg Dam

KORANNABERG

LANGBERG

1682m

Boegoeberg Dam

ASBESBERGE

R383

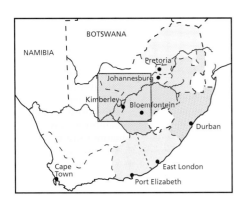

Kimberley and Bloemfontein

This semi-arid region of the country offers the visitor a number of interesting destinations located just outside the main centres of Kimberley (see page 62) and Bloemfontein (see page 59), as well as way beyond.

Located well to the northwest of Kimberley is Kuruman, one of Africa's most historically important mission stations. Situated close to the town is the Kuruman Nature Reserve which is a sanctuary for rhino, zebra and a variety of antelope.

Closer to Kimberley, just to the west, is the Vaalbos National Park, which features rhino, zebra, giraffe, springbok and a number of other antelope species.

A 20-minute drive to the south of Kimberley is Magersfontein, the site of one of the worst British defeats in the bitterly contested Anglo-Boer War in December 1899. The battlesite has a small museum and tearoom.

East of Bloemfontein is Thaba Nchu, the location of an attractive hotel and casino complex, as well as the Maria Moroka National Park which is home to a number of antelope species.

Three reserves north of Kimberley are worth visiting: the Willem Pretorius Game Reserve, a sanctuary proclaimed around the Allemanskraal Dam, and the Bloemhof Dam Nature Reserve and Sandveld Nature Reserve, these being situated at the top and bottom ends of the Bloemhof Dam.

Below: *By far the biggest tourist attraction in the historic town of Kimberley is the 'Big Hole' from which three tons of diamonds were dug before mining ceased here in 1914.*

KIMBERLEY	J	F	M	A	M	J	J	A	S	O	N	D
AVERAGE TEMP. °F	77	75	72	64	57	51	51	55	63	68	72	75
AVERAGE TEMP. °C	25	24	22	18	14	11	11	13	17	20	22	24
Hours of Sun Daily	10	9	9	9	9	9	9	10	10	10	10	10
RAINFALL in	2	2.5	3	1.5	0.5	0	0	0.5	1	1.5	2	
RAINFALL mm	61	65	73	42	19	7	7	9	13	28	43	52
Days of Rainfall	9	9	10	7	4	2	2	2	2	5	7	7

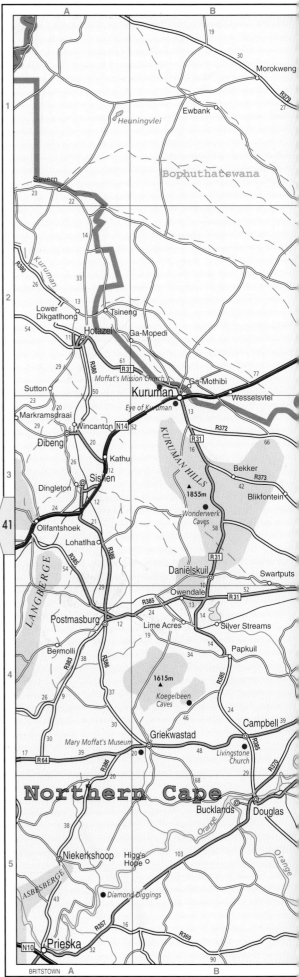

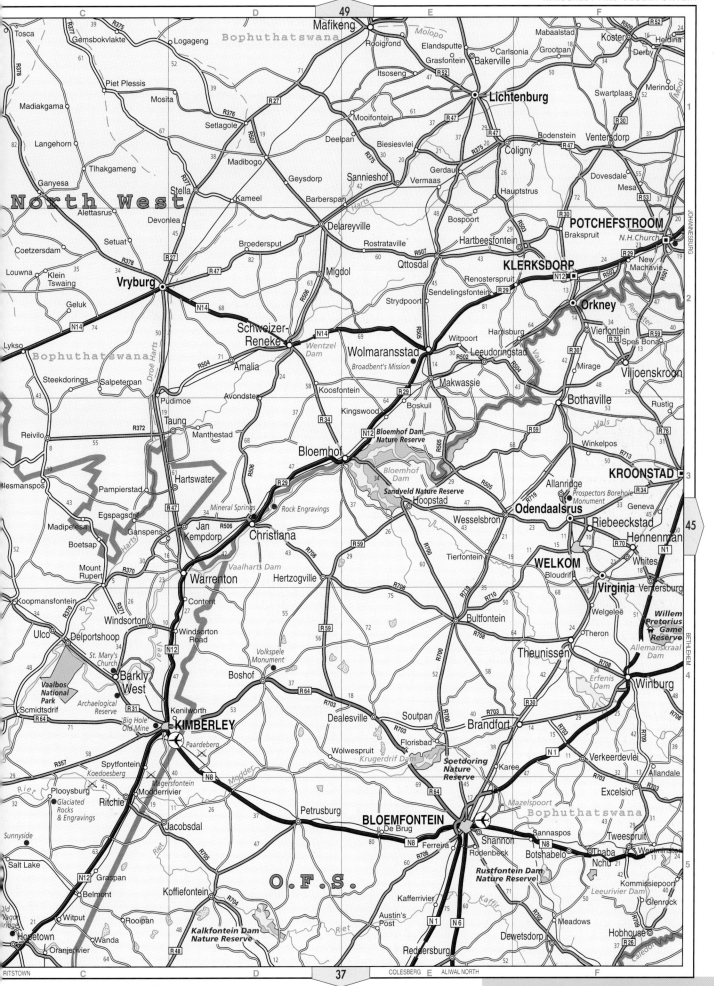

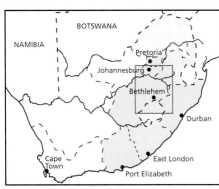

Northeastern Orange Free State

Although much of the Orange Free State is a flat, treeless expanse of grassland plain, the land in the eastern and southern part is much more scenically appealing, rising as it does in series of picturesquely weathered sandstone hills, and culminating in the southeastern corner in the impressive Maluti Mountains. The north-eastern Orange Free State is rich farmland and has bountiful mineral resources, and from the tourist's point of view, there are a number of natural attractions dotted over the area that are worth visiting.

The most visually attractive part of this region is undoubtedly the mountainous area found south of Bethlehem and Harrismith. One of the particular highlights of this area is the superb Golden Gate Highlands National Park, a 12,000-ha (29,500-acre) expanse of dramatically-sculpted sandstone ridges, peaks, cliffs, caves and weirdly-shaped formations. There is a large variety of antelope species in the park, as well as more than 160 species of bird. The Golden Gate has two rest camps offering self-contained accommodation, and there are facilities for horse riding, golf, trout-fishing and tennis.

The areas in and around the towns of Bethlehem and Harrismith have various natural attractions. Within the town of Bethlehem is the Pretoriuskloof Nature Reserve, and just to the south, the

Wolhuter Nature Reserve. Close to Harrismith are the Harrismith Botanic Gardens, with some interesting walks, and the Mount Everest Game Reserve.

Almost 100 km (62 miles) to the west of Bethlehem is the well-stocked Willem Pretorius Game Reserve, a 9,300-ha (23,000-acre) sanctuary on the Allemanskraal Dam. Numbered among the game are white rhino, giraffe, buffalo, wildebeest, many types of antelope and about 220 bird species. A public resort, established on a rocky hill overlooking the dam, offers self-contained accommodation and a variety of amenities. There are plenty of nature trails for hikers, and there is good angling on the dam.

One of the major recreational areas of the Orange Free State and the Transvaal is the Vaal River which forms a natural

boundary between the two regions. Its many resorts, caravan parks and camping grounds, set on the river's willow-shaded banks, provide a popular playground for thousands of holidaymakers and week-enders, mostly city folk from the Witwaters-rand. A particularly popular spot on the river is the Vaal Dam situated to the south-east of Vereeniging. It is ideal for a wide range of water sports and is much favoured by anglers.

Left: A Basotho tribesman, wearing traditional straw hat and blanket, stands in the foreground of one of the striking rock formations found in the Golden Gate area.

Top above : One of the Orange Free State's most important towns is Kroonstad where many of the buildings are constructed from the locally quarried sandstone.

Above: The Golden Gate Highlands National Park boasts some of the Orange Free State's most colourful and scenic vistas.

BETHLEHEM	J	F	M	A	M	J	J	A	S	O	N	D
AVERAGE TEMP. °F	68	67	64	57	50	44	44	48	55	61	63	66
AVERAGE TEMP. °C	19.9	19.4	17.9	13.9	10.0	6.5	6.6	9.1	13.3	15.9	17.6	19.2
Hours of Sun Daily	9	8	8	8	9	9	9	9	8	8	9	9
RAINFALL in	4.72	3.50	2.80	1.97	1.10	0.39	0.43	0.55	1.30	2.64	3.35	3.82
RAINFALL mm	120	89	71	50	28	10	11	14	33	67	85	97
Days of Rainfall	13	11	10	7	4	2	2	2	5	9	12	13

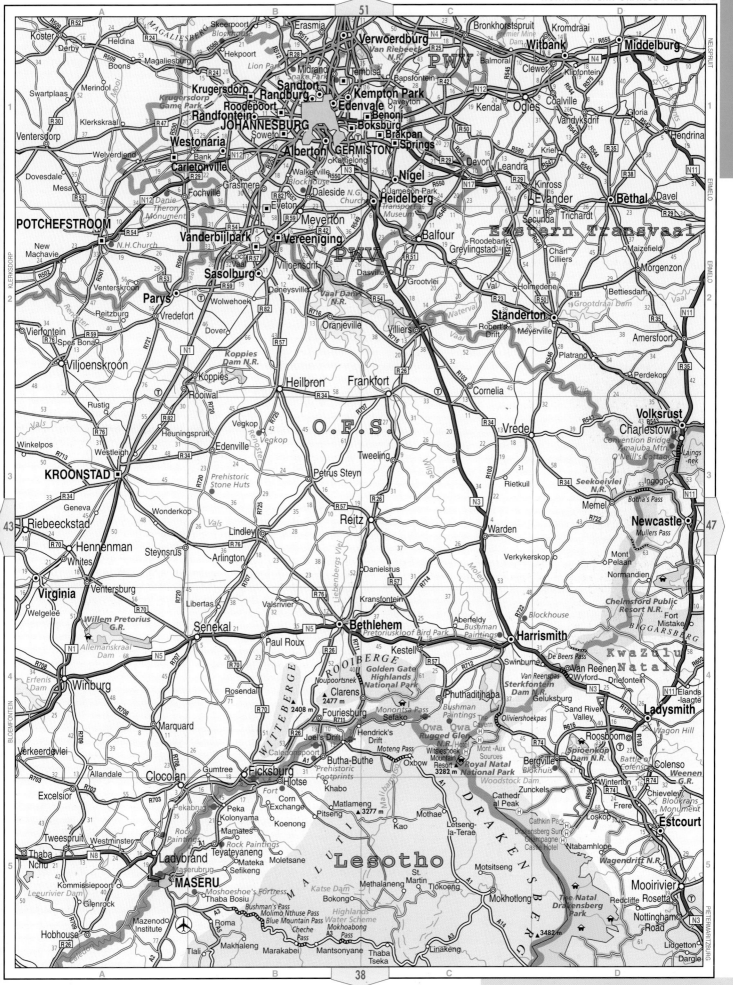

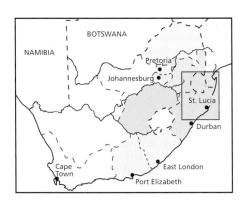

Northern KwaZulu Natal

A region of remarkable richness and diversity, northern KwaZulu Natal boasts four of South Africa's finest game reserves, and some of the world's great wetland and marine wilderness areas – Lake St Lucia and Maputaland further north. Much of the region is steeped in history and for much of the 19th century parts of it served as a bloody battleground: in 1818 Shaka's Zulu impis started fanning out to do battle with neighbouring peoples, then it was Voortrekkers pitted against the Zulus, and finally at the close of the century, the British fought here against the Boers. As a result, the area has many battlesites that can be visited.

From Eshowe to Ulundi, respectively the former capitals of Zululand and KwaZulu, a Zulu cultural route offers visitors authentic kraals and tangible reminders of past historical battles.

Inland, the Nkwaleni Valley is the location of Shakaland, originally created for the TV epic 'Shaka Zulu'. Situated one-and-a-half hours from Durban, this splendid complex comprises a kraal-type hotel in the form of a village of beehive huts. Attractions here include Zulu culinary specialities, traditional dancing, displays by sangomas (spirit mediums) and herbalists, basket-weaving, pot-making and hut-building.

On and around the coast is the Greater St Lucia Wetland Park, the centrepiece of which is Lake St Lucia, a beautiful estuarine system that is home to a myriad waterfowl, crocodile and hippo. Giant sea turtles use the beaches as breeding grounds. Among

visitor amenities are a variety of walking trails and excellent opportunities for game-viewing, bird-watching, boating, fishing, scuba-diving and snorkelling, as well as the interesting and informative Crocodile Centre. Accommodation at hotels and hutted rest camps can be arranged through the Natal Parks Board.

Further up the shoreline are two smaller but equally attractive stretches of water: Lake Sibaya (South Africa's largest freshwater lake) and Kosi Bay (a system of four lakes, and patches of mangrove swamp, as well as palm and sycamore fig forests), the latter situated close to the Mozambique border. Activities include fishing, bird-watching and turtle-viewing trips, and a variety of walking trails are offered.

Between the two lies the Maputaland Marine Reserve which boasts 20 different ecosystems, including three lake systems

which are home to hippo, crocodile and a superb array of birds. Magical Maputaland is considered to be one of the last undiscovered wilderness areas in southern Africa.

The various game areas in northern KwaZulu Natal are relatively small in size, but they are amongst Africa's finest. Of these is the Hluhluwe/Umfolozi Park. The Umfolozi section is a magnificent area of woodland savanna and flood plain and is best-known for its successful rhino conservation programme. The Hluhluwe section is a rich landscape of misty forests, grass-covered hills and dense thickets which sustain 84 mammal species – including rhino, elephant, giraffe and lion. Other notable reserves include Mkuzi, Itala, Ndumo and the Tembe Elephant Park.

For those interested in visiting the battlesites of yesteryear, the area east of Dundee contains three of the most significant: Blood River, where 10,000 Zulu warriors suffered an epic defeat at the hands of 486 Voortrekkers in 1838; Isandlwana and Rorke's Drift, where the British experienced defeat and victory against the Zulus in 1879; and Talana, where Boers defeated a British garrison during the first battle of the Anglo-Boer War in 1899.

Above: One of many historic monuments in South Africa – a 'laager' of 64 bronze oxwagons – is to be found at the Blood River battlesite in Northern KwaZulu Natal. It is a tangible reminder of the fierce struggle between the Boers, Zulus and British for possession of this beautiful land.
Right: Tourists can travel by launch around Lake St Lucia which lies at the heart of South Africa's largest wetland wilderness area.

Above: The Greater St Lucia Wetland Park is home to hundreds of different bird species, including the white pelican.

SWAZILAND

Eastern Transvaal

KwaZulu Natal

MBABANE

MAPUTO

Maputo Elephant Reserve

INDIAN OCEAN

Cabo de Santa Maria

Ponta Milibangalala

Ponta do Ouro

Kosi Bay Nature Reserve

Maputoland Marine Reserve

Sodwana Bay National Park

Greater St. Lucia Wetland Park

Lake St. Lucia

Cape Vidal

Leven Point

Jesser Point

Boteler Point

Hully Point

Mkuzi Game Reserve

Phinda Resource Reserve

St. Lucia Marine Reserve

Tembe Elephant Park

Ndumo G.R.

Pongolapoort Public Nature Reserve

Pongolapoort Dam

Lake Sibaya

Mbazwana

Sodwana Bay

Kosimeer

Emangusi

Ingwavuma

Lavumisa

Golela

Jozini

Candover

Ubombo

Mkuze

Pongola

Magudu

Mahlangasi

Nongoma

Hlabisa

Hluhluwe

Hluhluwe Dam

Hluhluwe Umfolozi Park

Hluhluwe / Umfolozi Park

Somkele

Mtubatuba

Riverview

Teza

St. Lucia Estuary

Dukuduku Forest Reserve

KwaMbonambi

Mzingazi Lake

Richards Bay Game Reserve

Richards Bay

Felixton

Empangeni

Umlalazi Nature Reserve

Mtunzini

Gingindlovu

aMatikulu

Mandini

Darnall

Tugela Mouth

Fort Pearson

Ultimatum Tree

Shaka's Memorial

Blythdale Beach

Shakaskraal

Aldinville

Stanger

Mapumulo

Sevenoaks

New Hanover

Dalton

Mpolweni

Howick

Albert Falls N.R.

Falls

Rietvlei

Craigie Burn Dam

Greytown

Ahrens

Kranskop

Muden

Eshowe

Nongqai Fort

Fort Mtombeni

Fort Kwa-Mondi

Hinza Forest Reserve

Entumeni

Coward's Bush Monument

Cetshwayo's Grave

Site of Shaka's Kraal

The Ranch

Keate's Drift

Tugela Gorge

Tugela Ferry

Pomeroy

Helpmekaar

Isandhlwana

Rorke's Drift

Vant's Drift

Nqutu

Babanango

Ulundi

Ondini

Ulundi Piet Retief's Grave

Mgungundlovu

Dingaan's Kraal

Mangeni

Silutshana

Elandskraal

Randalhurst

Osborn

Nkandla

Quden

Dlolwana

Melmoth

Mtonjaneni

Ndundulu

Nkwalini

Mahlabatini

Nhlazatshe

Swart Umfolozi

Black Umfolozi

White Umfolozi

Gluckstadt

Calvert

Where Prince Imperial died

Battle of Talana

Glencoe

Dundee

Wasbank

Hattingspruit

Dannhauser

Kingsley

Bloedrivier

Scheepersnek

Raadsaal and Fort of New Republic

Steilrand

Ngome

Ngobeni

Hlobane

Louwsburg

Itala N.R.

Bivane

Hot Springs

Mpemvana

Paulpietersburg

Grootspruit

Groenvlei

2277 m

BALELESBERG

Utrecht

Vryheid

Madadeni

Osizweni

P.L. Uys Memorial

Van Rooyen

Bloedrivier

Nondweni

Wakkerstroom

Pongola Bush N.R.

Luneberg

Dirkiesdorp

Bergen

Commondale

Berbice

Onverwacht

Mahamba

Mineral Bath

Piet Retief

Anysspruit

Bothashoop

Hlathikhulu

Gege

Kubutsa

Sithobela

Maloma

Nhlangano

Mhlosheni

Hluthi

Nsoko

Big Bend

Siphofaneni

Mkhaya Nature Reserve

Sidvokodvo

Mpaka Stn.

Siteki

Mafutseni

Manzini

Loyengo

Mankayane

Houtkop

Sicunusa

Bushman Paintings

Mhlambanyatsi

Bhunya

Nerston

Amsterdam

Sheepmoor

Panbult

Iswepe

Ngwempisi

Lothair

Holbank

Ermelo

Breyten

Chrissies-meer

Warburton

Carolina

Belfast

Dalmanutha

Grobler's brug

Machadodorp

Mineral Springs

Badplaas

Barberton

Saddleback

Josefsdal

Bulembu

Nelsbergpas

Jambila

Bothasnek

Noordkaap

Avoca

Old Stock Exchange

Piggs Peak

Bushman Paintings

Malolotja Nature Reserve

Lochiel

Oshoek

Hartbeeskop

Forbes Reef

Lundzi

Waverley

Croydon

Swazi Market

Mlilwane Game Reserve

Lobamba

King's Village

Mafutseni

Mpaka Stn.

Ngonini

Matsamo

Hereford

Sihove

Border Gate

Tshaneni

Mhlume

Lomahasha

Goba

Tabankulu

Mlawula N.R.

Hlane Game Sanct.

Changalane

Bela Vista

Salamanga

Zitundo

Manhoca

Catuane

LEBOMBO

LEBOMBOBERG

KaNgwane

Jeppe's Reef

Nelspruit

Moamba

Vundica

Mevedja

Marracuene

Chicabela

Machava

Boane

Catembe

Louis Trichardttrek Memorial

Inhaca

Ponta de Macaneta

Incomati

Komati

Lusutfu

Usutu

Mkhondvo

Ngwavuma

Mkuze

Pongola

Bivane

Sundays

Tugela

Umvoti

Black Umfolozi

White Umfolozi

RICHARDS BAY	J	F	M	A	M	J	J	A	S	O	N	D
AVERAGE TEMP. °F	78	78	77	73	68	63	63	66	69	71	73	77
AVERAGE TEMP. °C	25	25	25	22	20	17	17	19	20	21	23	25
Hours of Sun Daily	7	7	7	8	8	7	8	8	7	6	7	7
SEA TEMP. °F	75	75	75	73	71	70	68	68	68	70	70	73
SEA TEMP. °C	24	24	24	23	22	21	20	20	20	21	21	23
RAINFALL in	5.5	5.5	4	4	5	1	2	2.5	3.5	3.5	3.5	3
RAINFALL mm	144	138	110	111	126	31	47	59	84	97	97	83
Days of Rainfall	12	10	9	8	9	6	6	8	9	10	12	10

47

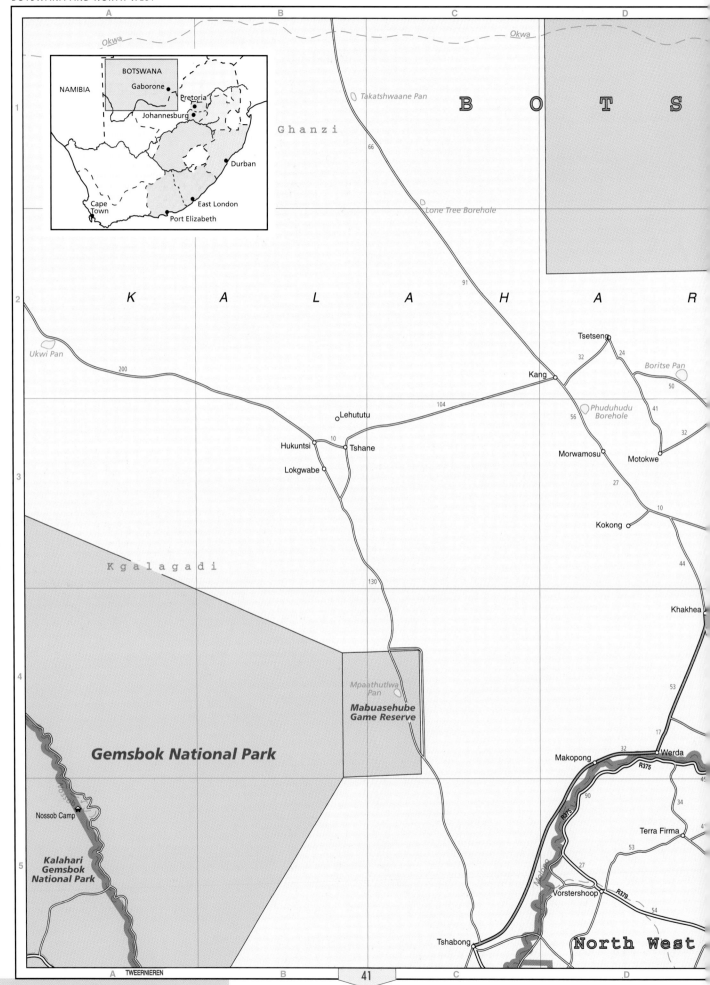

BOTSWANA

NAMIBIA

Gaborone

Pretoria

Johannesburg

Durban

Cape Town

East London

Port Elizabeth

Okwa

Okwa

Takatshwaane Pan

Ghanzi

B O T S

66

Lone Tree Borehole

91

K A L A H A R

Tsetseng

32

24

Boritse Pan

Ukwi Pan

200

Kang

104

50

Phuduhudu Borehole

41

56

32

Lehututu

10

Hukuntsi

Tshane

Morwamosu

Motokwe

Lokgwabe

27

10

Kokong

Kgalagadi

44

130

Khakhea

Mpaathutlwa Pan

53

Mabuasehube Game Reserve

17

Gemsbok National Park

Makopong

32

Werda

R375

45

R375

90

34

Nossob

Terra Firma

Nossob Camp

53

Kalahari Gemsbok National Park

Molopo

27

Vorstershoop

R379

54

Tshabong

North West

TWEERNIEREN

Ghanzi

W A N A

Central Kalahari Game Reserve

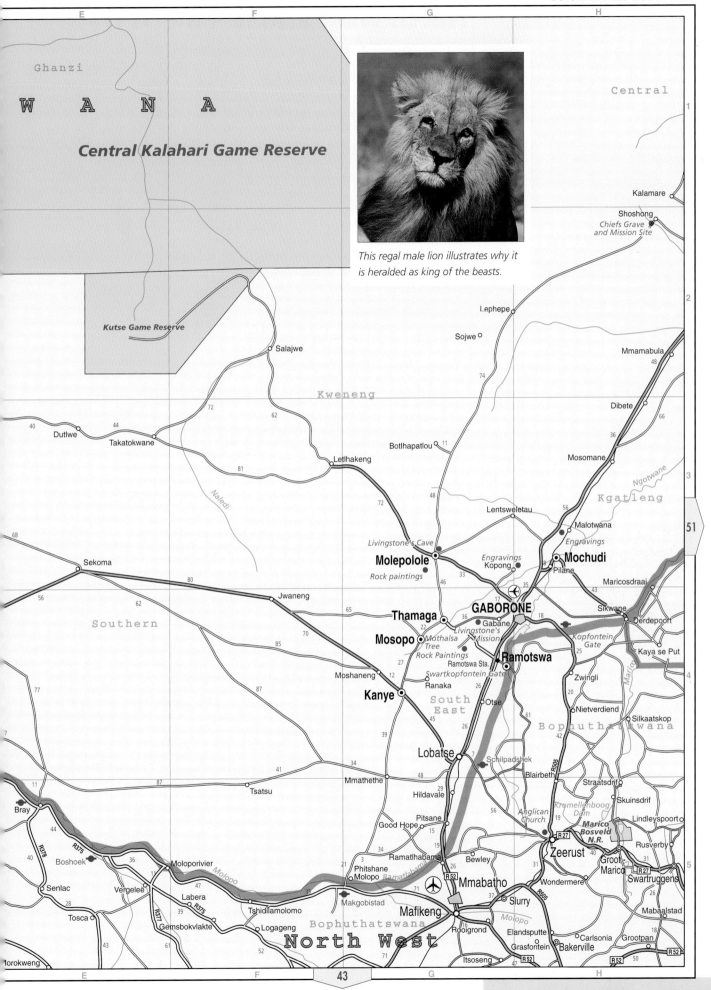

This regal male lion illustrates why it is heralded as king of the beasts.

Central

Kalamare

Shoshong
*Chiefs Grave
and Mission Site*

Kutse Game Reserve

Lephepe

Sojwe

Mmamabula
48

Salajwe

Kweneng

74

72

62

Dibete

66

40

44

Dutlwe

Takatokwane

Botlhapatlou 11

Mosomane

36

81

Ngotwane

Letlhakeng

Kgatleng

72

48

Naledi

Lentsweletau

56

68

Malotwana

Engravings

Sekoma

80

Livingstone's Cave

Engravings
Kopong

Molepolole

Mochudi
8

Maricosdraai

Rock paintings

46

33

Pilane

43

Jwaneng

35

Sikwane

56

62

65

Thamaga

36

GABORONE
17

18

Derdepoort

70

Gabane

*Livingstone's
Mission*

Mosopo

*Mothalsa
Tree
Rock Paintings*

*Kopfontein
Gate*

85

27

Ramotswa Sta.

Ramotswa

25

Kaya se Put

Southern

Moshaneng

12

Swartkopfontein Gate

Zwingli

77

Ranaka

26

20

Kanye

South
East

Otse

Nietverdiend

Silkaatskop

87

39

26

61

Bophuthatswana

7

Lobatse

42

34

7

Schilpadshek

Straatsdrif

41

48

Mmathethe

Blairbeth

Skuinsdrif

11

29

Hildavale

56

*Kromellenboog
Dam*

Lindleyspoort

Bray

Pitsane

*Anglican
Church*

19

Rusverby

44

Good Hope

15

*Marico
Bosveld
N.R.*

40

R378

36

Boshoek

34

19

Bewley

Zeerust

40

Groot-
Marico

31

R27

Swartruggens

Senlac

1

Moloporivier

21

3

Ramatlhabama

R52

Mmabatho

Wondermere

26

Vergelee

47

Phitshane
Molopo

71

37

Slurry

Mabaalstad

28

Labera

Molopo

Makgobistad

Mafikeng

Slurry

18

Tosca

39

Tshidilamolomo

Bophuthatswana

Rooigrond

Elandsputte

Carlsonia

Grootpan

R52

Logageng

North West

Grasfontein

Bakerville

R52

43

52

71

Itsoseng

47

R52

50

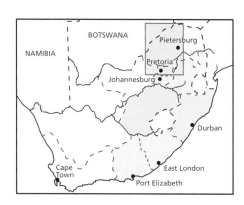

North West and Northern Transvaal

This northern corner of South Africa is a vast, hot, flattish country of bushveld and thorn, of lonely farmsteads shaded by eucalyptus and bright green willow trees, of fields of sunflowers and groundnuts, tobacco and citrus and villages that sleep soundly in the sun. Here one finds one of the great granaries of southern Africa, with endless fields of maize stretching out to the furthest horizons. Scattered across this wide expanse are a number of natural and man-made attractions that are well worth travelling out from the main centres of Pretoria and Johannesburg to visit.

Undoubtedly the top tourist attraction of this area is Sun City – an enormous, extravagently opulent complex of hotels, gaming rooms, theatres, restaurants, bars, discos and shops, all set in spacious and beautifully landscaped grounds. The gem of the complex is the Palace of the Lost City, an ornate affair of domes and minarets which was the venue of the Miss World beauty pageant in 1993. Among Sun City's attractions is the Valley of the Waves, an outdoor playground incorporating waterfalls, lakes, river rides and an enormous pool with artificially generated waves. For golfers, Sun City offers an Arizona desert-style golf course where crocodiles lie in wait at the 13th hole, and another course at the Gary Player Country Club, the venue of the annual Million Dollar Golf Challenge.

Situated to the north of Sun City is the Pilanesberg National Park, a great expanse of game-rich habitat that sprawls within four concentric mountain rings, relics of an aeons-old volcano. Some 10,000 head of game are found in the park, among them both the black and white rhino, giraffe and zebra, as well as more than 300 bird species. The park is traversed by an extensive network of game-viewing roads.

The Great North Road (N1) leading from Pretoria offers a number of interesting places to visit. Warmbad (Warmbaths), 93 km (58 miles) north, is renowned for its curative springs. The Hydro Spa, situated here, compares with the best in the world.

Near the small centre of Naboomspruit about 60 km (37 miles) further on are two excellent bird sanctuaries which offer a wide and diverse range of species: the Trans-Oranje Bird Sanctuary and the Mosdene private reserve.

A further 51 km (32 miles) north is the Potgietersrus Nature Reserve, a somewhat unusual wildlife enterprise that serves as a breeding unit for exotic and local wildlife species – including llama, pygmy hippo and white and black rhino.

Top left: An old whitewashed church contrasts with the backdrop of modern commercial buildings in the Northern Transvaal's principal town of Pietersburg.
Bottom left : The Hartbeespoort Dam, situated to the west of Pretoria, attracts thousands of watersports enthusiasts over the weekends.
Below: The spectacular Palace hotel, part of the multimillion-dollar Lost City complex.

PIETERSBURG	J	F	M	A	M	J	J	A	S	O	N	D
AVERAGE TEMP. °F	73	72	70	65	59	54	54	58	63	68	70	72
AVERAGE TEMP. °C	22	22	20	18	15	12	12	14	17	20	21	22
Hours of Sun Daily	8	8	8	8	9	9	9	9	9	9	8	8
RAINFALL in	3.5	2.5	2	1	0	0	0	0	0.5	1.5	3	3.5
RAINFALL mm	91	72	61	31	11	4	5	4	14	41	80	91
Days of Rainfall	10	8	8	5	3	1	1	1	2	6	10	10

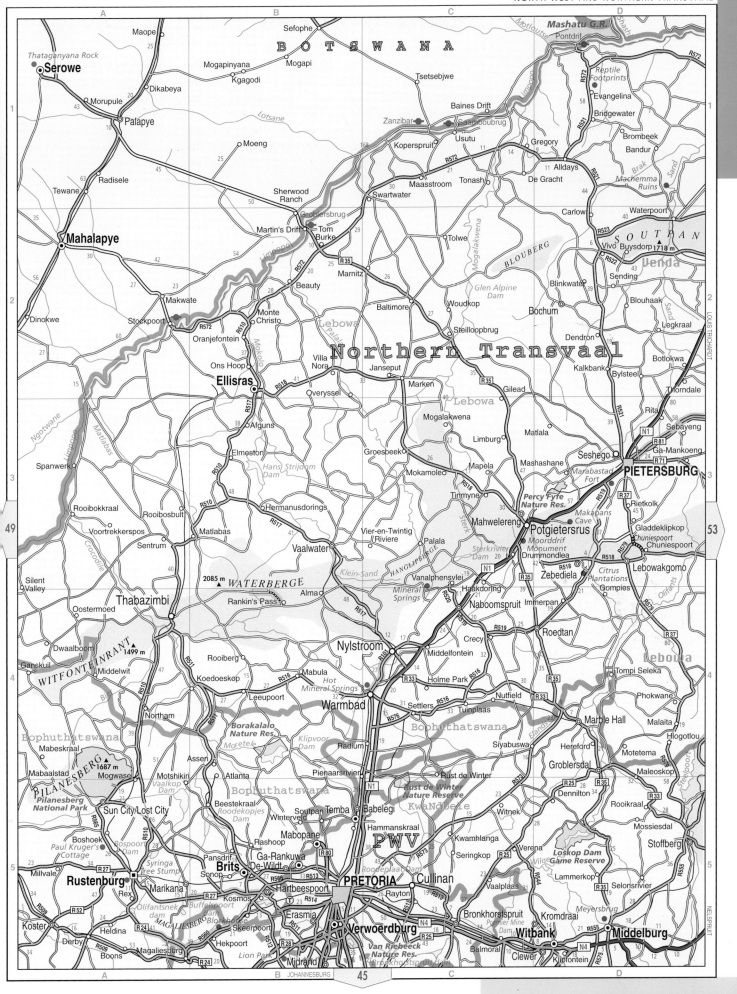

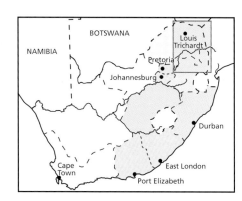

Eastern and Northern Transvaal

Much of the Eastern and Northern Transvaal area is dominated by the Great Escarpment, a spectacular compound of forest-mantled mountains, deep ravines, crystal streams and delicate waterfalls. For sheer scenic beauty, few other parts of the country can compare with this imposing range which rises near Nelspruit and runs north-eastwards for some 300 km (186 miles). To the east of the Escarpment is the game-rich Lowveld, on which the vast expanse of the Kruger National Park and numerous other game reserves are situated (see page 14).

There's no shortage of exciting destinations in this area, two of the best being the Blyde River Canyon and Pilgrim's Rest.

Blyde River Canyon is one of Africa's great natural wonders: a massive and majestic red-sandstone gorge whose cliff faces plunge almost sheer to the waters below. The 20-km (12-mile) long gorge has been dammed to create a lovely lake, and at the top of the canyon there are strategically sited viewing points, easily reached from the main road. There is a reptile park close by, and the reserve above the gorge offers rewarding walks, hiking trails and bridle paths for horse riding.

The town of Pilgrim's Rest was born out of a gold rush that began in the 1870s. Although gold is no longer mined here, the town continues to prosper as a 'living museum', its early character wonderfully preserved. Tourists can sleep in rooms that are much as they were a century ago; there are guided tours around the village and the interesting Diggers' Museum offers gold-panning demonstrations.

Situated about 70 km (43 miles) south of Pilgrim's Rest are the magnificent Sudwala Caves, a complex of underground caverns festooned with cream-coloured stalactites and stalagmites. Nearby is the Dinosaur Park, an unusual and fascinating open-air display featuring life-sized replicas of the giant reptiles that ruled the earth about 250 million years ago.

A bit further to the southeast is Nelspruit, the main centre of the Eastern Transvaal (see page 68).

The principal town of the Northern Transvaal is Pietersburg which has a particularly impressive nature reserve close by.

A bit further to the east is Tzaneen, which lies at the heart of the fertile Letaba district, and just to the west of Tzaneen are the misty, thickly-wooded heights of the Magoebaskloof in which large tracts of indigenous forest are to be found.

To the northeast is Modjadji, royal residence of the mysterious Rain Queen. Part of her domain is a forest of thousands of cycads – the largest concentration of these ancient plants in the world.

Below left: One of the most fascinating sights to be found in the Blyde River Canyon area is Bourke's Luck Potholes, an intriguing fantasia of hollowed-out rocks.

Below: Much of Pilgrim's Rest consists of historic miners' cottages, such as the two seen here – one of which has been turned into a handicrafts shop.

NELSPRUIT	J	F	M	A	M	J	J	A	S	O	N	D
AVERAGE TEMP. °F	75	74	73	69	63	59	59	63	66	70	72	73
AVERAGE TEMP. °C	24	24	29	21	18	15	15	7	20	21	22	23
Hours of Sun Daily	7	7	7	7	8	8	9	9	8	7	6	6
RAINFALL in	5	5	4	2	1	0.5	0.5	0.5	11	2.5	4.5	5
RAINFALL mm	130	119	98	47	19	10	10	10	29	65	114	13
Days of Rainfall	13	12	10	7	4	2	3	3	5	9	13	13

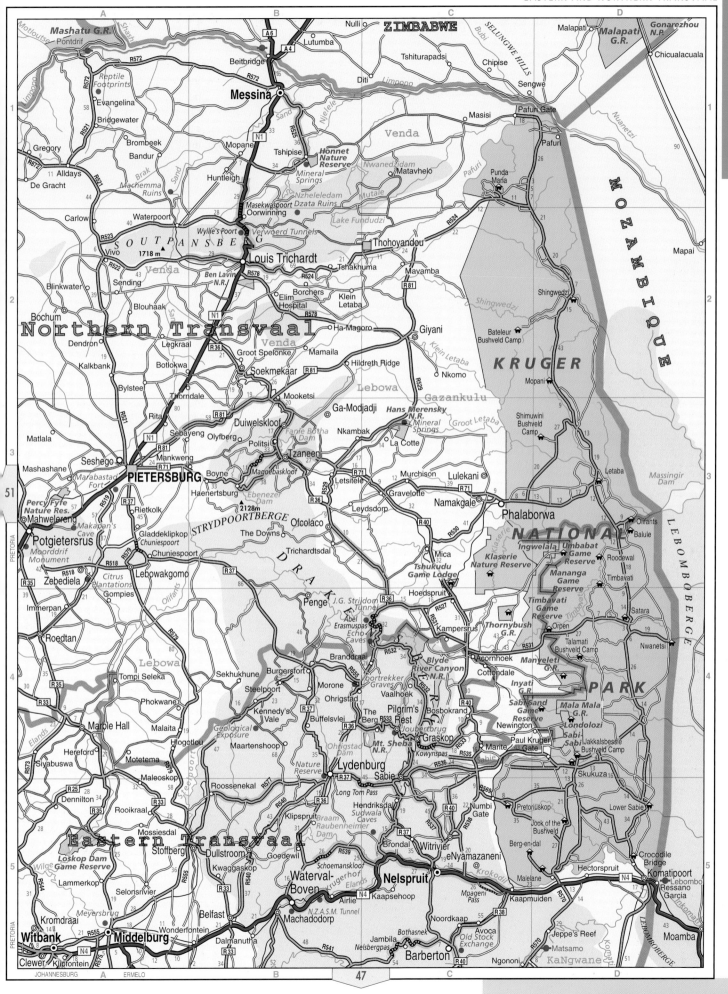

Town Plans Key and Legend

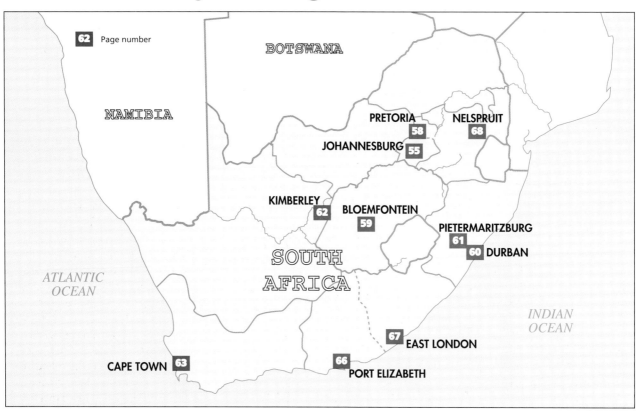

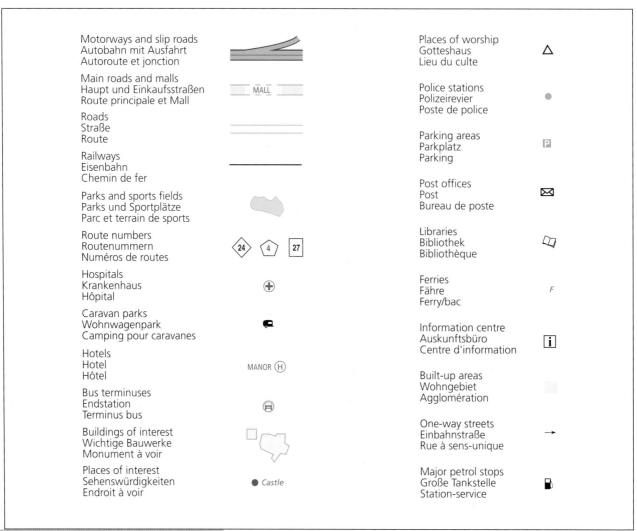

English	German	French	Symbol
Motorways and slip roads	Autobahn mit Ausfahrt	Autoroute et jonction	
Main roads and malls	Haupt und Einkaufsstraßen	Route principale et Mall	MALL
Roads	Straße	Route	
Railways	Eisenbahn	Chemin de fer	
Parks and sports fields	Parks und Sportplätze	Parc et terrain de sports	
Route numbers	Routenummern	Numéros de routes	24 4 27
Hospitals	Krankenhaus	Hôpital	
Caravan parks	Wohnwagenpark	Camping pour caravanes	
Hotels	Hotel	Hôtel	MANOR (H)
Bus terminuses	Endstation	Terminus bus	
Buildings of interest	Wichtige Bauwerke	Monument à voir	
Places of interest	Sehenswürdigkeiten	Endroit à voir	• Castle
Places of worship	Gotteshaus	Lieu du culte	△
Police stations	Polizeirevier	Poste de police	•
Parking areas	Parkplatz	Parking	P
Post offices	Post	Bureau de poste	✉
Libraries	Bibliothek	Bibliothèque	
Ferries	Fähre	Ferry/bac	F
Information centre	Auskunftsbüro	Centre d'information	i
Built-up areas	Wohngebiet	Agglomération	
One-way streets	Einbahnstraße	Rue à sens-unique	→
Major petrol stops	Große Tankstelle	Station-service	

Johannesburg City Centre

Johannesburg is South Africa's largest city as well as its industrial, commercial and financial capital. It is packed with fine hotels and restaurants, shopping malls, galleries, museums and theatres, and has a vibrancy and uninhibited zest for life that is reflected in the social as well as the business scene. The heart of the city is in many ways a microcosm of the country, a cultural kaleidoscope of past and future. Here, postmodern towers are juxtaposed with a few stately survivors of the city's gold rush days, while along the city's pavements vendors jostle noisily for business.

A good place from which to get your bearings on 'The Golden City' is Carlton Panorama, the observation deck situated on the 50th floor of the Carlton Centre in Commissioner Street. Also on offer here are a gold exhibition and two sound and light shows.

Travel west along Commissioner Street from the Carlton Centre and you'll find Diagonal Street with its gleaming skyscrapers, one of which houses the Johannesburg Stock Exchange where free weekday tours are offered.

North of the city centre, located on either side of Jan Smuts Avenue, is the Johannesburg Zoo. It is home to more than 3,000 animals, birds and reptiles, 30 of which are listed as endangered species. Zoo Lake features an illuminated fountain and attracts boaters, picknickers, strollers and those who simply want to laze in the sunshine.

Johannesburg boasts scores of different museums and galleries. Notable among these are: the MuseumAfrica (corner of Wolhuter and Bree streets), which explores both the culture and history of the people of South Africa; the Planetarium (Yale Road, Braamfontein) where the wonders of star travel can be experienced in armchair comfort; the Transnet Museum (Old Station concourse in De Villiers Street) which covers the whole public-transport scene from steam railways to airways and harbours; the Museum of Military History (next to the zoo) which has a splendid expo of militaria, with special emphasis on the two world wars; and the Johannesburg Art Gallery (Joubert Park), which includes collections of South African, English, French and Dutch works.

An evocative reconstruction of the old pioneer days of Victorian Johannesburg is to be found at the 'living museum', Gold Reef City, situated south of central Johannesburg (see page 10).

JOHANNESBURG	J	F	M	A	M	J	J	A	S	O	N	D
AVERAGE TEMP. °F	68	67	65	60	55	50	51	55	61	63	65	67
AVERAGE TEMP. °C	20	20	18	16	13	10	10	13	16	18	18	19
Hours of Sun Daily	8	8	8	8	9	9	9	10	9	9	8	8
RAINFALL in	5	4	3	2	1	0.5	0.5	0.5	1	3	4	4
RAINFALL mm	131	95	81	55	19	7	6	6	26	72	114	106
Days of Rainfall	15	11	11	9	4	2	1	2	3	10	14	14

Above left: The Johannesburg city centre – financial and industrial heart of the country – viewed from the Berea.
Left: Horse-drawn carriage rides can be enjoyed at Gold Reef City.

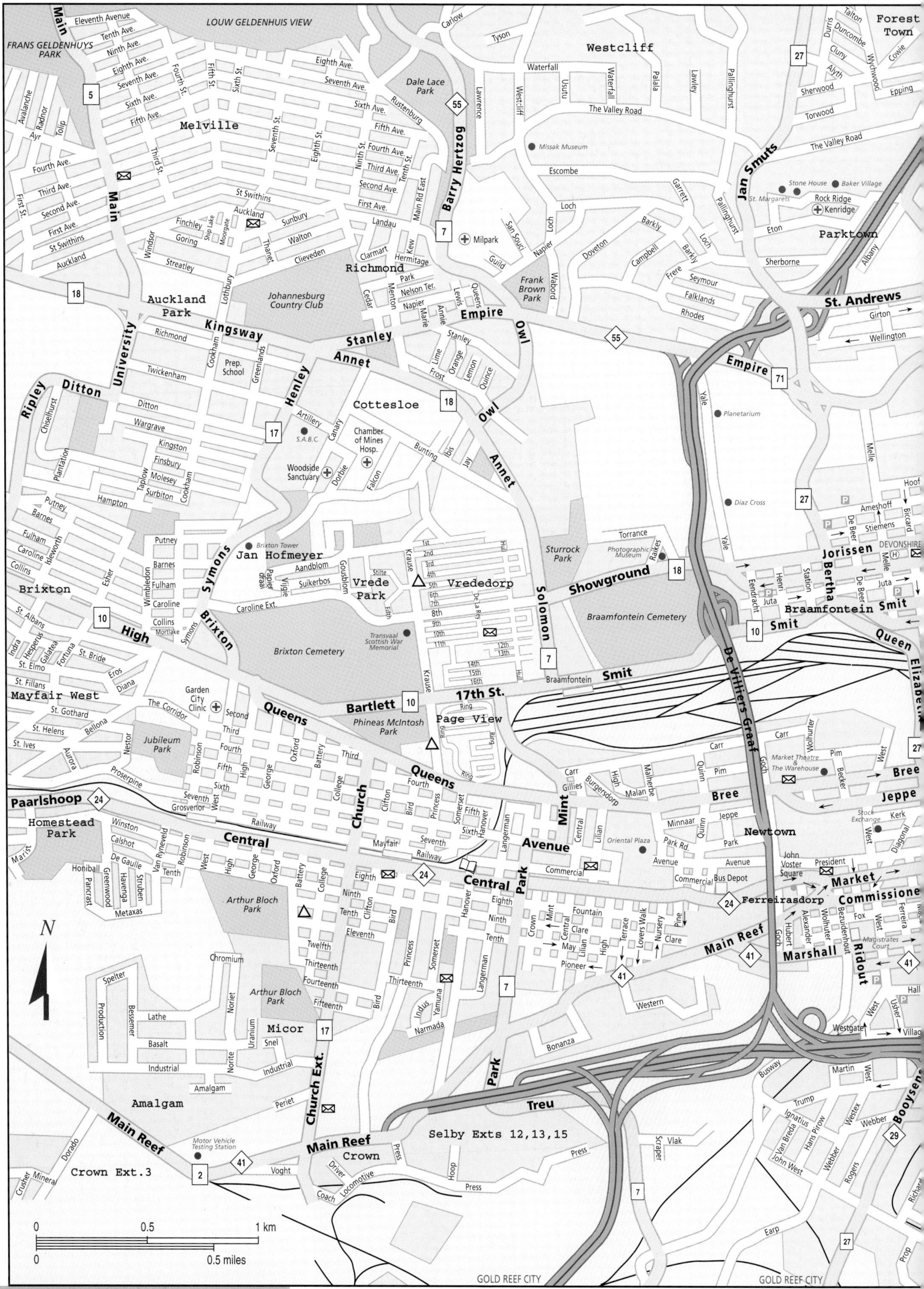

Westcliff
Forest Town
Melville
Parktown
Richmond
Auckland Park
Cottesloe
Jan Hofmeyer
Vrede Park
Vrededorp
Brixton
Mayfair West
Page View
Homestead Park
Newtown
Ferreirasdorp
Micor
Amalgam
Crown
Crown Ext.3
Selby Exts 12,13,15
LOUW GELDENHUIS VIEW
FRANS GELDENHUYS PARK
Dale Lace Park
Johannesburg Country Club
Prep. School
Frank Brown Park
Sturrock Park
Braamfontein Cemetery
Brixton Cemetery
Transvaal Scottish War Memorial
Phineas McIntosh Park
Jubileum Park
Arthur Bloch Park
Missak Museum
Stone House
Baker Village
St. Margarets
Rock Ridge
Kenridge
Milpark
Chamber of Mines Hosp.
Woodside Sanctuary
S.A.B.C.
Brixton Tower
Planetarium
Diaz Cross
Photographic Museum
Garden City Clinic
Market Theatre & The Warehouse
Stock Exchange
Oriental Plaza
John Voster Square
Bus Depot
Magistrates Court
Motor Vehicle Testing Station
DEVONSHIRE
GOLD REEF CITY
Main
Barry Hertzog
Jan Smuts
Kingsway
Stanley
Annet
Empire
Owl
St. Andrews
University
Ditton
Ripley
Henley
Symons
Brixton
High
Queens
Bartlett
17th St.
Solomon
Showground
Smit
Jorissen
Bertha
Braamfontein
Queen Elizabeth
De Villiers Graaf
Bree
Jeppe
Market
Commissioner
Marshall
Ridout
Central
Avenue
Mint
Park
Church
Church Ext.
Paarlshoop
Main Reef
Treu
Booysens
The Valley Road
0
0.5
1 km
0
0.5 miles
N

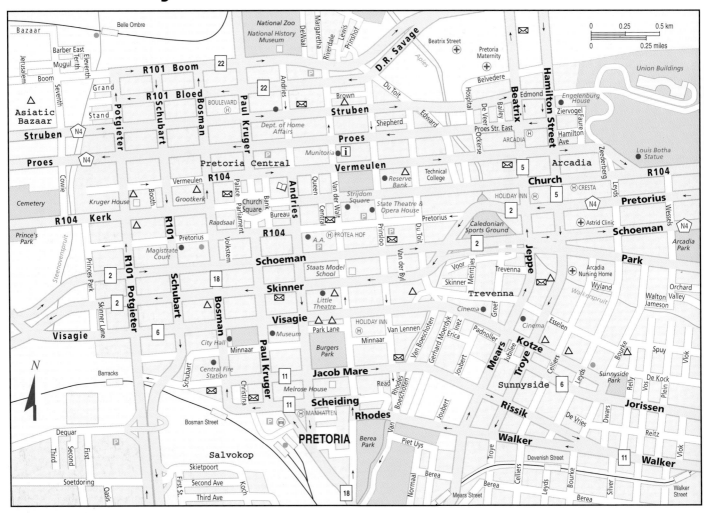

Pretoria is a handsome city noted for its stately and historic buildings, its parks and gardens, its splendid wealth of indigenous flora and for its jacarandas. Some 80,000 of these exquisite trees grace the open areas and line the streets. Pretoria's informal name – the 'Jacaranda City' – derives from their lilac-blossomed glory in springtime (October). The city is the administrative capital of the country and is also an important national centre of research and learning.

Pretoria's famed jacaranda trees turn the streets of the city into a glorious blaze of lilac during the spring months of October and November. The first two jacarandas were imported from Rio de Janeiro in 1888 and planted in the suburb of Sunnyside where they thrived.

One of Pretoria's greatest tourist attractions is its zoo, one of the biggest in the world and home to about 3,500 exotic and indigenous animals. These include the four great apes, the rare South American maned wolf, a white tiger, and the only known giant eland in captivity in Africa. An aerial cableway takes visitors to the summit of a hill, from where they can view the wildlife in its natural habitat. There is also an excellent reptile house and aquarium where visitors can watch seals being fed in the mid-morning and mid-afternoon.

Situated at the heart of Pretoria is Church Square. Among the more prominent buildings here are the Old Raadsaal (parliament) and the graceful Palace of Justice. The square's northern frontage is vaguely reminiscent of the Place de la Concorde in Paris, while its southern frontage reminds one of London's Trafalgar Square. Dominating the square is the imposing bronze statue of Paul Kruger, generally regarded as the 'Father of Afrikanerdom'.

One of the most impressive and visible architectural sights in Pretoria is the Union Buildings. Designed by Sir Herbert Baker, this magnificent, crescent-shaped, neo-classical complex looks out over the city from the heights of Meintjies Kop. The beautifully landscaped and terraced grounds are open to the public.

PRETORIA	J	F	M	A	M	J	J	A	S	O	N	D
AVERAGE TEMP. °F	73	73	71	64	59	53	54	59	65	68	70	73
AVERAGE TEMP. °C	23	22	21	18	15	11	12	14	18	20	21	22
Hours of Sun Daily	9	8	8	8	9	9	9	10	10	9	9	9
RAINFALL in	6	3	3	2	0.5	0	0	0.5	2.5	4	4	4
RAINFALL mm	152	76	80	57	14	3	3	6	21	67	101	10
Days of Rainfall	14	11	10	7	3	1	1	2	3	8	12	14

Bloemfontein City Centre

Bloemfontein – also known as Mangaung, meaning place of the cheetah – is the judicial capital of South Africa and the principal city of the Orange Free State. The most centrally situated of South Africa's major cities, it lies at the heart of an area of fertile farmland 1,392 m (4,567 ft) above sea level and owes its prosperity to the Free State goldfields located 160 km (100 miles) to the northeast. The city is particularly noted for its impressive buildings, museums, monuments and memorials.

BLOEMFONTEIN	J	F	M	A	M	J	J	A	S	O	N	D
AVERAGE TEMP. °F	73	71	67	59	52	45	45	50	58	63	68	72
AVERAGE TEMP. °C	23	21	19	15	11	7	7	10	14	17	19	22
Hours of Sun Daily	10	9	9	9	9	9	9	9	10	10	10	10
RAINFALL in	3.5	4	3	2	0.5	0.5	0	0.5	0.5	1.5	2	2.5
RAINFALL mm	91	99	74	58	21	12	9	14	19	42	59	62
Days of Rainfall	11	10	11	8	4	2	2	3	8	7	8	9

The City of Bloemfontein has many historic buildings, one of the finest being the classical Fourth Raadsaal, which was completed in 1893.

The finest views of Bloemfontein can be obtained from the top of Naval Hill. Some 200 ha (494 acres) of this hill consist of the Franklin nature reserve which is home to a number of game species, such as eland, springbok, red hartebeest, blesbok and Burchell's zebra. At the foot of Naval Hill, in Union Avenue's Hamilton Park, is the Orchid House, within which are pools, bridges, waterfalls, weathered stone and over 3,000 exquisite orchids.

Situated along Kingsway is King's Park, the city's principal public garden. The park incorporates Loch Logan (a largish lake), the zoo (animals include a large number of monkeys), and a magnificent rose garden with more than 4,000 rose trees. (The best months to see the roses are October and November.) King's Park is the venue for an open-air market, held on the first Saturday of each month.

One of the most impressive of the city's monuments is the National Women's Memorial in Monument Road. It was built in memory of the nearly 27,000 Boer women and children who died (mainly of disease) in British concentration camps during the Anglo-Boer War which took place around the turn of the century. Of related interest is the nearby Military Museum of the Boer Republics.

The city's most venerable structure, the Old Raadsaal, reflects the classical revival: Greek in detail and Renaissance in form.

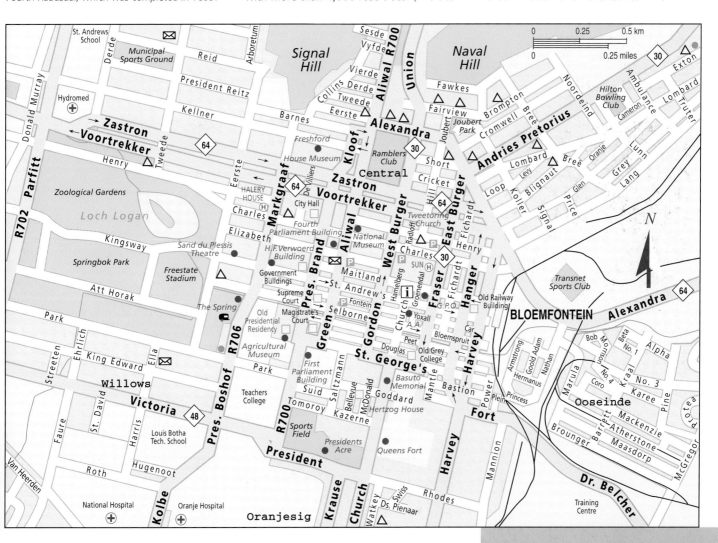

Durban City Centre

The city of Durban is the country's third largest metropolis and foremost seaport; in fact, it's the biggest and busiest harbour in Africa. With its fine beaches and excellent tourist amenities, Durban is one of the country's most popular holiday destinations. It is especially famous for its excellent watersporting facilities: its beaches offer some of the best surfing venues in the country, and deep-sea game-fishing trips, scuba diving and sailing trips are all readily available to the tourist. The Botanic Gardens, featuring an orchid house, is one of the many 'green' spaces in the greater Durban area.

Durban's popular North Beach, seen here against a backdrop of high-rise luxury apartments, offices and hotel blocks, is a magnet to thousands of sunworshippers and pleasure-seekers in the summer, especially in the holiday months of December and January.

Durban's beachfront, known as the 'Golden Mile', is the city's leading tourist attraction. This holiday playground stretches 6 km (4 miles) along the sandy Indian Ocean shoreline and offers everything in the way of entertainment: paddling pools, pavilions, piers, amusement parks, round-the-clock eating places and nightclubs, entertainment centres, colourful markets and broad thoroughfares that lead past some of Africa's most elegant hotels. However, it is the broad sweeping beaches along the 'Golden Mile' that are the prime attraction.

Among the more popular drawcards on the 'Golden Mile' are Sea World, an aquari-um and dolphinarium at the bottom end of West Street, and the Fitzsimon's Snake Park (Snell Parade) which has a fine collection of exotic and indigenous species, including crocodiles, leguaans (iguanas) and terrapins. Also on the 'Golden Mile', a few blocks in from the beachfront, is one of Durban's newest and most vibrant shopping complexes, The Wheel.

A few blocks to the west of the city centre is a colourful and exotic world of mosques and temples. The focal point is the Victoria Street Indian Market, a large and busy place of bargain and barter housed in a huge domed building.

DURBAN	J	F	M	A	M	J	J	A	S	O	N	D
AVERAGE TEMP. °F	76	76	75	71	66	62	62	63	66	69	72	74
AVERAGE TEMP. °C	24	25	24	22	19	17	16	17	19	20	22	23
Hours of Sun Daily	6	7	7	7	7	7	7	7	6	5	5	6
SEA TEMP. °F	75	77	75	73	70	68	66	66	68	70	72	73
SEA TEMP. °C	24	25	24	23	21	20	19	19	20	21	22	23
RAINFALL in	5	4	5	3	3	1	2	2	3	4	4	4
RAINFALL mm	135	114	124	87	64	26	44	58	65	89	104	108
Days of Rainfall	15	12	12	9	7	5	5	7	10	14	16	15

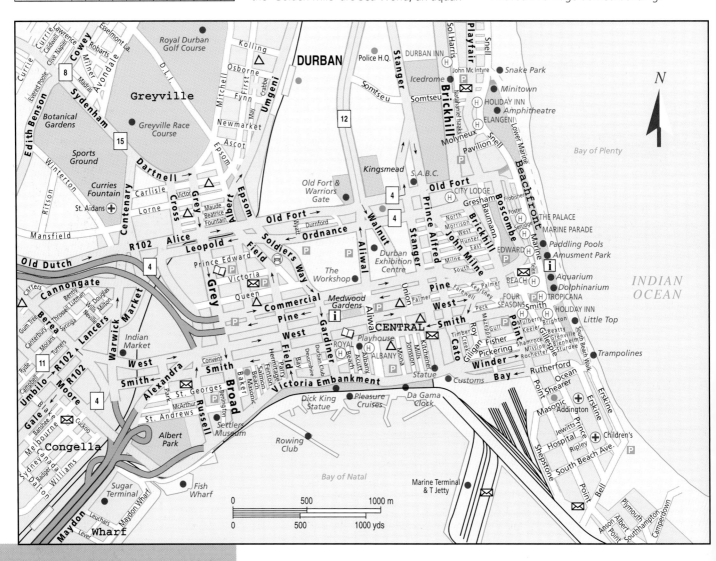

Pietermaritzburg City Centre

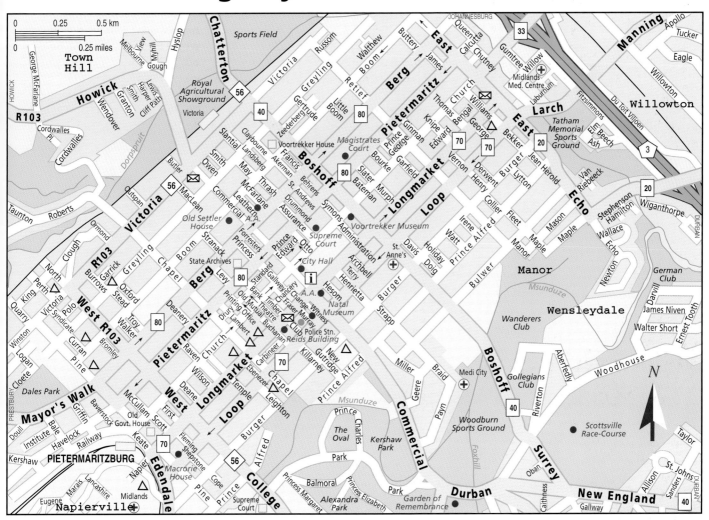

Lovely red-brick Victorian buildings, cast-iron railings and store-fronts, luxuriant parks and gardens bright with roses and azaleas, antique shops and bookstores, and a charming historic air that draws much from a very colonial past – this is Pietermaritzburg, the province's administrative centre. Nestling in a hollow among green and sometimes misty hills, just under 100 km (62 miles) from Durban, Pietermaritzburg not only has a lot to offer the discerning visitor, it is also an ideal base from which to explore the interior of KwaZulu Natal, especially the lovely countryside of the Midlands.

Pietermaritzburg was founded by the Boer Voortrekkers in 1838 and its Trekker origins can be seen in the Church of the Vow, a small, gabled edifice erected to commemorate the defeat of the mighty Zulu army at Blood River; it now serves as the Voortrekker Museum.

However, the town's history and character are distinctly British colonial rather than Afrikaner, its Victorian heritage on display in the Macrorie House Museum and in the delightful collection of 1850s shops and houses that are part of the Natal Museum.

Other reminders of the past include the Old Natal Parliament and the City Hall. The latter, an imposing affair of domes, stained glass and a clock tower, is the southern hemisphere's largest all-brick building.

Central Lanes – bounded by Longmarket, Timber and Church streets and Commercial Road – is a charming network of narrow pedestrian alleys that once functioned as the city's financial and legal centre. Notable are the small speciality shops and the elegantly Edwardian Harwin's Arcade.

Pietermaritzburg is known as the 'City of the Flowers' and deservedly so. Its floral glory is at its best in springtime; the annual flower show is held in September. A number of gentle, two-hour Green Belt walking trails enable visitors to enjoy some of the lovely countryside that fringes the city.

Alexandra Park has wonderful displays of aloes and roses, and the Botanic Gardens features an 'international section' of exotics and spring displays of azaleas and camelias.

Above: *Pietermaritzburg is renowned for its outstanding examples of Victorian architecture. The bandstand in Alexandra Park, with its intricate cast-iron railings, is typical of buildings constructed during that era.*

PIETERMARITZBURG	J	F	M	A	M	J	J	A	S	O	N	D
AVERAGE TEMP. °F	73	73	72	66	60	54	55	58	63	66	68	72
AVERAGE TEMP. °C	23	23	22	19	16	12	13	15	17	19	20	22
Hours of Sun Daily	6	7	7	7	7	7	7	7	6	5	5	6
RAINFALL in	5.5	4.5	4.5	1.5	1	0	0	1	2.5	3	3.5	4.5
RAINFALL mm	137	115	109	45	26	12	12	31	65	75	97	110
Days of Rainfall	18	15	15	10	5	3	3	5	10	15	19	19

Kimberley City Centre

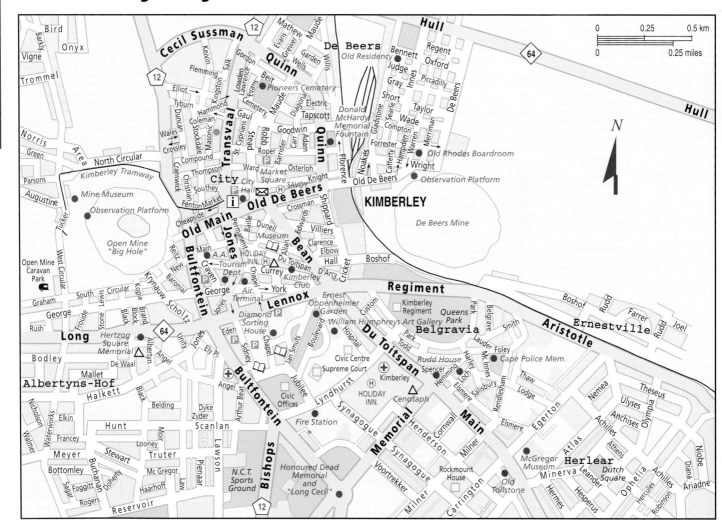

Mention the name Kimberley to a South African and one word immediately comes to mind – diamonds. This town was brought to birth in the 1870s when tens of thousands of prospectors poured into the area to unearth the sought-after glittering gems that lay in abundance beneath the dusty ground. Today, Kimberley still retains much of the old-world atmosphere of these heady days when instant fortunes were made (and lost) and money and champagne flowed like water.

KIMBERLEY	J	F	M	A	M	J	J	A	S	O	N	D
AVERAGE TEMP. °F	77	75	72	64	57	51	51	55	63	68	72	75
AVERAGE TEMP. °C	25	24	22	18	14	11	11	13	17	20	22	24
Hours of Sun Daily	10	9	9	9	9	9	9	10	10	10	10	10
RAINFALL in	2	2.5	3	1.5	0.5	0	0	0	0.5	1	1.5	2
RAINFALL mm	61	65	73	42	19	7	7	9	13	28	43	52
Days of Rainfall	9	9	10	7	4	2	2	2	2	5	7	7

The Diggers Fountain in the Oppenheimer Memorial Gardens honours the thousands of miners, past and present, who helped create Kimberley, the Diamond City.

The historic hub of Kimberley is the 'Big Hole', until recently the world's largest man-made crater. At the height of the diamond rush more than 30,000 miners could be seen working cheek by jowl in its depths. By 1914, when it finally closed down, the hole had reached a depth of more than 1,000 m (3,280 ft) and yielded a staggering three tons of diamonds.

Beside the 'Big Hole' (now largely filled with water), and providing an evocative and comprehensive insight into the town's lively past, is the Kimberley Mine Museum. Part of the museum consists of a very authentic re-creation of part of the early town. The museum complex also includes the De Beers Hall, which houses diamond displays, among them finished jewellery stones of various and attractive colours, and the world's largest uncut diamond (616 carats); the Transport Hall, which holds some splendid Victorian vehicles; and the Art Gallery which profiles the various and fascinating faces of Kimberley during the 19th century.

Other notable museums and galleries in Kimberley are the Duggan-Cronin Gallery (Egerton Road), the McGregor Museum (Egerton Road), the Old Museum (Chapel Street), and the William Humphreys Art Gallery (situated in the Civic Centre), while stately period homes like a Rudd House in Loch Road and Dunluce in Lodge Road reflect a grand past.

Cape Town City Centre

The central metropolitan area of Cape Town huddles in the 'bowl' formed by majestic Table Mountain, its flanking peaks and the broad sweep of Table Bay. Founded by the first Dutch settlers who landed here in 1652, Cape Town is the country's oldest city and the fourth largest in terms of population. More than 300 years of history have given it its unique character – a rich and vibrant blend of English, Dutch, French and Malay influences. It is an attractive, colourful city that boasts excellent hotels and restaurants, open-air markets and shops catering for every pocket and taste.

Fortunately for visitors, the compactness of central Cape Town makes it ideal for exploring on foot. A pleasant morning's walk could start in St George's Mall, a nine-block, brick-paved pedestrian walk-way lined with shops and arcades and enlivened by umbrella-shaded bistros and buskers. Close to this mall is the vast and glittering complex of shops, restaurants and cinemas known as the Golden Acre.

Situated at the top end of the mall is St George's Cathedral, and behind it lies the beautifully maintained and laid out Public Gardens. The Houses of Parliament and Tuynhuys can be seen on the left as you walk up the central, oak-lined Government Avenue; towards the top of the Gardens on the left is the National Gallery and Jewish Museum, and to the right, the South African Museum and Planetarium.

An absolute must on any visitor's agenda is the Victoria and Alfred Waterfront, a multibillion-dollar venture that has borrowed ideas from San Francisco's harbour project. Among its many varied attractions are restaurants, bistros and bars, speciality shops, craft, fish and fresh produce markets, cinemas, theatres, hotels, museums and a historic walk.

The city's most notable landmark is the Castle, situated next to the Grand Parade. This massive, pentagonal fortress was designed to defend the fledgling Dutch colony from assault from both land and sea. Today it serves as a museum and offers guided tours five times daily.

CAPE TOWN	J	F	M	A	M	J	J	A	S	O	N	D
AVERAGE TEMP. °F	70	70	69	63	58	55	54	55	57	61	64	68
AVERAGE TEMP. °C	21	21	20	17	15	13	12	13	14	16	18	20
Hours of Sun Daily	11	10	9	7	6	6	6	7	8	9	10	11
SEA TEMP. °F	59	57	55	55	54	54	54	55	55	57	57	67
SEA TEMP. °C	15	14	13	13	12	12	12	13	13	14	14	14
RAINFALL in	1	1	1	2	3	4	3	3	2	2	1	1
RAINFALL mm	14	17	19	39	74	92	70	75	39	37	15	17
Days of Rainfall	5	4	5	8	12	12	11	13	10	8	5	5

Above top: *The city of Cape Town viewed from the top of Table Mountain, which is easily accessible by means of a cablecar.*
Above: *South Africa's stately Houses of Parliament, originally constructed in 1884, overlook the Cape Town Gardens; the public is allowed to sit in the parliamentary gallery during sessions.*
Right: *Vibrant and colourful, the Coon Carnival is part of traditional New Year celebrations in the Cape. Troupes of brightly clad musicians dance and sing through the streets of Cape Town.*

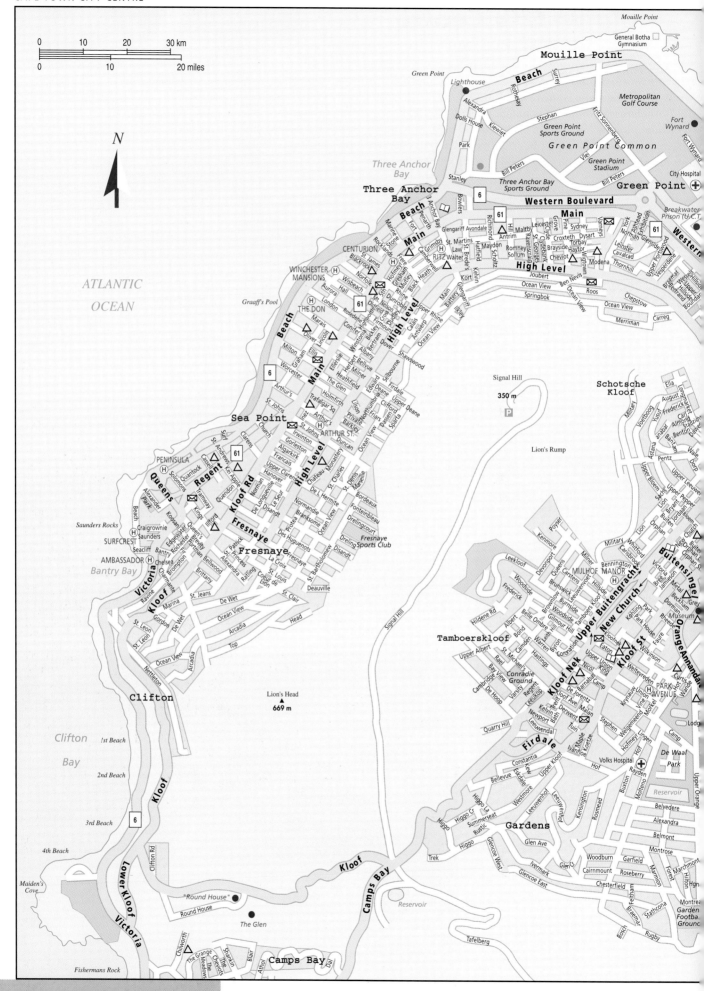

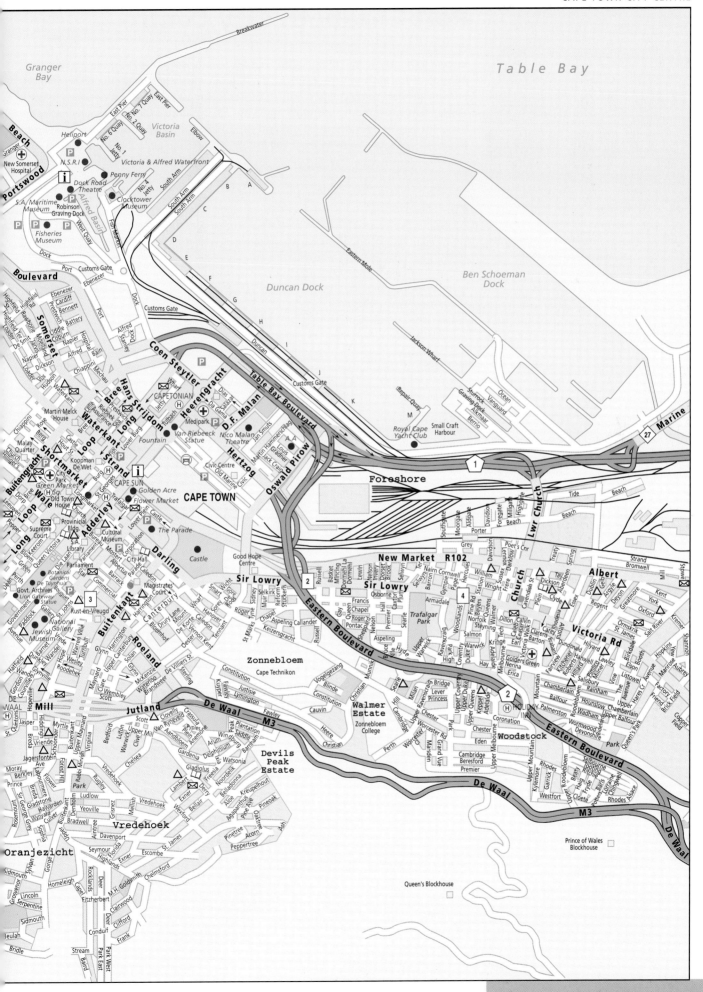

Port Elizabeth City Centre

Known variously as the 'friendly city' and the 'windy city', Port Elizabeth is the economic hub of the Eastern Cape; much of the industrial activity of this area being connected with the vehicle-assembly sector. 'P.E.' – as it is most often called – is also a major tourist centre. Set on the shores of Algoa Bay, the country's fifth largest city has some excellent beaches, historic buildings and various sophisticated shopping centres. Port Elizabeth owes its origins to the 4,000 British settlers who landed here in 1820.

A statue of Queen Victoria – a remnant of the British Empire – gazes out from the foreground of Port Elizabeth's grand old Public Library building. The city was established by the British settlers who landed at Algoa Bay in 1820. The acting governor of the Cape at the time, Sir Rufane Donkin, named the fledgling township Port Elizabeth in memory of his young wife who had died of fever in India two years before.

PORT ELIZABETH	J	F	M	A	M	J	J	A	S	O	N	D
AVERAGE TEMP. °F	70	70	69	65	61	58	57	57	60	62	65	68
AVERAGE TEMP. °C	21	21	20	18	16	14	14	14	15	17	18	20
Hours of Sun Daily	9	8	7	7	7	7	7	8	7	8	9	7
SEA TEMP. °F	70	70	68	66	63	61	61	61	63	64	66	70
SEA TEMP. °C	21	21	20	19	17	16	16	16	17	18	19	21
RAINFALL in	2	2	2	2	3	2	2	3	3	2	2	1
RAINFALL mm	41	39	55	57	68	61	54	75	70	59	49	34
Days of Rainfall	2	8	10	9	9	8	8	10	9	11	11	9

Port Elizabeth has four major beaches: King's, Humewood, Hobie and Pollok. The first comprises long stretches of golden sands, swimming pools, a miniature railway and an entertainment amphitheatre; the second is linked with the sheltered Happy Valley area, with its picnicking lawns, lily ponds and riverside paths. Colourful Hobie Beach is the scene of Hobie Cat sailing, rubber-ducking and various beach sports; a thriving fleamarket crowds the promenade above the sand at weekends. Finally, Pollok beach is a popular venue for surfers.

The city's biggest tourist attraction is its Oceanarium and Museum Complex at Humewood. Trained dolphins play to the gallery, with Cape fur seals and jackass penguins also getting in on the act. The complex includes an impressive snake park where visitors can see some 80 snake species, as well as crocodiles, leguaans, and other reptiles. Snake-handling demonstrations are held daily. The Tropical sector contains a 'night-house', colourful birds and other wildlife in a jungle-like environment.

The city's main shopping area is the central business district's Market Square and Main Street; along the western parts of Main are several buildings with upstairs' malls, such as Traduna Mall which lies off Market Square. There are inviting speciality shops in Rink Street, Parliament Street and at Walmer Park.

The city's most historically important building, built in 1799, is Fort Frederick in Belmont Terrace overlooking the Baakens River estuary. It is open to the public on weekdays.

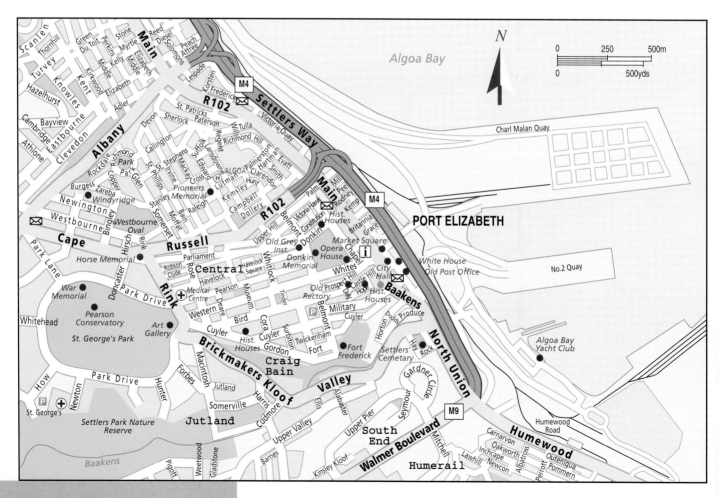

East London City Centre

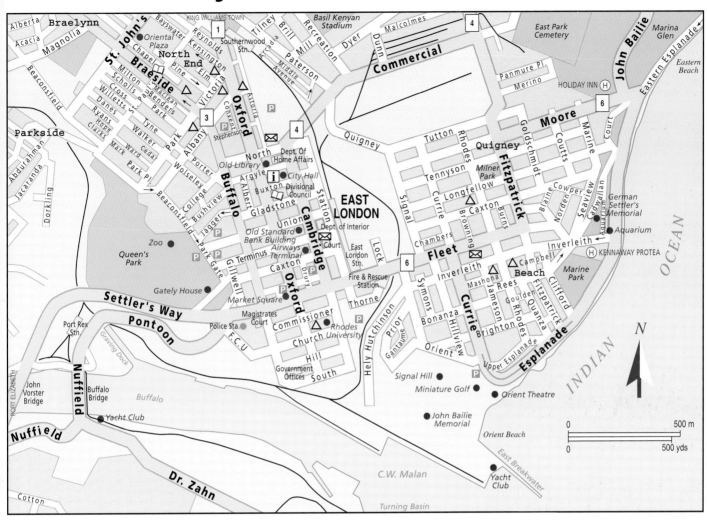

Situated at the mouth of the Buffalo River, the river-port of East London combines the charm of a relatively small community with all the essential amenities of a large city. Its attractions are of the quiet, undemanding, family-orientated kind: it has fine beaches, pleasant parks and gardens, good hotels and restaurants, and some fairly entertaining nightlife in the summer months along the seafront. Oxford Street is the principal thoroughfare along which you'll find modern shops, many of them catering to the tourist.

EAST LONDON	J	F	M	A	M	J	J	A	S	O	N	D
AVERAGE TEMP. °F	71	72	70	67	63	61	60	61	62	64	66	69
AVERAGE TEMP. °C	22	22	21	19	17	16	15	16	16	17	19	20
Hours of Sun Daily	7	7	7	7	7	7	8	7	7	7	7	8
SEA TEMP. °F	66	66	66	64	64	63	63	63	63	64	64	64
SEA TEMP. °C	19	19	19	18	18	17	17	17	17	18	18	18
RAINFALL in	3	4	4	3	2	1.5	2	3	3.5	3.5	3.5	3
RAINFALL mm	74	95	106	80	55	40	51	75	93	95	90	74
Days of Rainfall	13	12	12	9	9	5	5	7	9	13	12	12

Yachts at anchor on the Buffalo River which flows into the sea at East London.

One of East London's great attractions is its superb beaches, the most popular and easily accessible one being Orient Beach. Bounded by the 2-km (1.2-mile) Esplanade, it features the promenade pier, Orient Theatre and a restaurant.

Well worth a visit is the East London Museum in Oxford Steet. Its most notable exhibit is the first coelacanth to be caught in modern times (this primitive fish was thought to have become extinct 60 million years ago). Other displays are devoted to enthnology, prehistory and local history.

Situated on the Esplanade is an aquarium featuring about 400 marine species. Seal shows are held twice daily and are very popular, especially with children.

The Queen's Park botanical gardens, situated along Settler's Way and Beaconsfield roads, display some attractive indigenous flora. The park also has a zoo with more than 1,000 animals in residence, and there are pony rides for children.

Other places of interest include: Gately House in Queen's Street, one of the East Bank's first private homes and now part of the Museum complex; the Ann Bryant Gallery off Oxford Street (between St Mark's and St Luke's roads) which exhibits some final local paintings and sculptures; and the German Settler Memorial, an impressive work on the Esplanade which commemorates the arrival of more than 3,000 German immigrants in 1858.

Nelspruit Town Centre

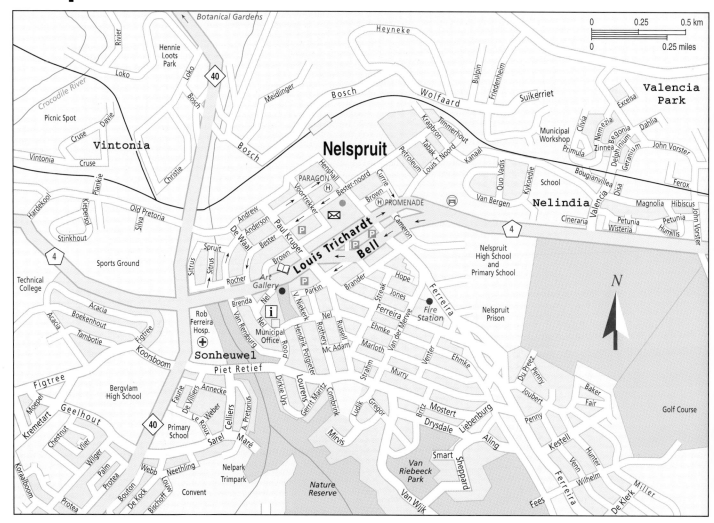

Nelspruit, the capital town of the Eastern Transvaal, is a pleasant, prosperous-looking place of clean-lined buildings, wide streets and tree-garlanded suburbs. It's the last major centre on the main west–east highway from Johannesburg and Pretoria (the N4) and the jumping-off point for tourists arriving by both road and air (it has a small but modern airport). The countryside around the town is delightful, especially along the immensely fertile Crocodile River Valley – a major citrus-growing region.

NELSPRUIT	J	F	M	A	M	J	J	A	S	O	N	D
AVERAGE TEMP. °F	75	74	73	69	63	59	59	63	66	70	72	73
AVERAGE TEMP. °C	24	24	29	21	18	15	15	7	20	21	22	23
Hours of Sun Daily	7	7	7	8	8	9	9	8	7	6	6	
RAINFALL in	5	5	4	2	1	0.5	0.5	0.5	11	2.5	4.5	5
RAINFALL mm	130	119	98	47	19	10	10	10	29	65	114	13
Days of Rainfall	13	12	10	7	4	2	3	3	5	9	13	13

Surrounded by scented orange groves and dominated by a cluster of granite domes, the town of Nelspruit is one of the most attractive centres in the Eastern Transvaal. Its avenue-like streets are shaded by poinciana trees which burst into blazing colour during the summer months of December and January.

There are good hotels and restaurants in and around town and some sophisticated shops; curios, handwoven rugs, carvings and leather goods are on sale in specialist outlets and in the larger stores; fresh produce in season, including a choice of tropical fruit, is sold by the many farm stalls along the region's roads.

Among Nelspruit's many attractions are the Lowveld Botanic Gardens. Sited on the banks of the Crocodile River, it is a haven for a fascinating variety of Lowveld floral species – about 500 of them. Of interest – to the layperson as well as the botanist – is the adjacent Lowveld Herbarium. A walk through the gardens will bring you to the Cascades viewsite, a platform overlooking the rocks and river.

One of the most attractive buildings in Nelspruit is the imposing town hall. Situated on an island just outside the hall is an unusual sundial in the shape of a wagon wheel – a memorial to the early Voortrekkers who in the early 19th century made their way through this area into Mozambique in search of a route to the sea.

The lush, verdant growth of the Transvaal Lowveld is evident at the Lowveld Botanical Gardens where more than 500 floral species are found.

Index

Aalwynsfontein D2 34
Aandster D3 43
Aansluit H2 41
Abbotsdale B4 32
Aberdeen C5 37
Aberfeldy C4 45
Acornhoek C4 53
Adams Mission F2 39
Addo E2 33
Adelaide F5 37
Adendorp D5 37
Afguns B3 51
Aggeneys D1 34
Agter Sneeuberg D4 37
Albertinia E4 33
Alberton B1 45
Alderley D5 38
Aldinville beach G1 39
Alettasrus C2 43
Alexander Bay A4 40
Alexandria F2 33
Alheit F4 41
Alice F1 33
Alicedale E1 33
Aliwal North F3 37
Allandale F4 43
Allanridge F3 43
Alldays D1 51
Amalia D2 43
Amanzimtoti F2 39
Amatikulu G1 39
Amersfoort D2 45
Amsterdam A2 47
Andrieskraal D2 32
Andriesvale F2 41
Anysberg D4 32
Anysspruit A2 47
Ariamsvlei E3 41
Arlington B3 45
Aroab E2 41
Ashton C4 32
Askeaton B4 38
Askham F2 41
Askraal D4 32
Assen B4 51
Aston Bay D2 32
Atlanta B4 51
Atlantis B4 32
Aurora D5 34
Aus A2 40
Austin's Post E1 36
Avoca A1 47
Avondrust D3 32
Avontuur B2 32
Babanango B4 47
Badplaas A1 47
Bain's Drift C1 51
Bakerville E1 43
Balfour C2 45
Balfour F5 37
Ballito G2 39
Baltimore C2 51
Bandur D1 51
Bank B1 45
Banner Rest F3 39
Bapsfontein C1 45
Barakke D5 37
Barberton A1 47
Barkly East C3 38
Barkly East C4 43
Barkly Pass C3 38
Barrington A2 32
Barrydale D4 32
Bashee Bridge C4 38
Beacon Bay G1 33
Beafort West A5 26
Beauty B2 51
Bedford E5 37
Beestekraal B5 51

Behulpsaam D5 37
Beitbridge B1 53
Bekker B3 42
Bela Vista D2 47
Belfast A1 47
Bell G1 33
Bellevue E1 33
Bellville B4 32
Belmont C1 36
Benoni C1 45
Berbice B3 47
Berea C4 32
Bergen A2 47
Bergrivier A3 32
Bergville D4 45
Berlin G1 33
Bermolli A4 42
Berseba B1 40
Bethal D1 45
Bethanie B2 40
Bethel B5 38
Bethelsdorp D2 32
Bethlehem B4 45
Bethulie E2 37
Bettiesdam D2 45
Betty's Bay B5 32
Bewley G5 49
Bhunya B2 47
Biesiesvlei E1 43
Big Bend C2 47
Bisho G1 33
Bisi E3 39
Bitterfontein D3 34
Bivane B3 47
Bizana E3 39
Bladgrond E4 43
Blairbeth H5 49
Blanco A2 32
Blesmanspos C3 43
Blinkfontein B3 42
Blinkwater D2 51
Blinkwater F5 37
Bloedrivier A4 47
Bloemfontein F1 36
Bloemhoek E1 35
Bloemhof E3 43
Blouberstrand B4 32
Bloudrif F3 43
Blouhaak D2 51
Bluegums B3 38
Blythdale beach G1 39
Bo-Wadrif F5 35
Boane D1 47
Bochum D2 51
Bodenstein F1 43
Boerboonfontein D4 32
Boetsap C3 43
Bokfontein B3 32
Bokhara F3 41
Boknesstrand F2 33
Bokong D1 38
Boksburg B1 45
Bolo Reserve B5 38
Bolotwa B4 38
Bonekraal G4 35
Bonnievale C4 32
Bonny Ridge E3 39
Bontrand E3 39
Borchers B2 53
Bosbokrand C4 53
Boshof D4 43
Bospoort E2 43
Bossiekom F1 35
Bothaville F3 43
Botlhapatlou G3 49
Botlokwa D2 51
Botrivier B5 32
Botshabelo F1 36
Boyne B3 53
Braemar F2 39
Brakpan C1 45
Branddraai C4 53
Brandfort F4 43

Brandkop E3 35
Brandrivier E4 33
Brandvlei F2 35
Brandwag F4 33
Braunschweig G1 33
Braunville B4 38
Bray E5 49
Breakfast Vlei F1 33
Bredasdorp C5 32
Breidbach G1 33
Breipaal F2 37
Breyten A1 47
Bridgewater D1 51
Brits B5 51
Britstown B3 36
Broedersput D2 43
Brombeek D1 51
Bronkhorstspruit C1 45
Brooks Nek E3 39
Bruintjieshoogte D5 37
Bucklands C1 36
Buffelsdrif A2 32
Buffelsvlei B4 53
Bulembu A1 47
Bulletrap C1 34
Bultfontein E4 43
Bulwer E2 39
Buntingville D4 38
Burgersdorp F3 37
Burgersfort B4 53
Butha-Buthe B4 45
Butterworth C5 38
Buysdorp D2 51
Bylstee D2 51
Cala C4 38
Caledon C5 32
Calitzdorp E4 33
Calvert A4 47
Calvinia F4 35
Cambria C2 32
Cameron Glen E5 37
Campbell B4 42
Camperdown F2 39
Cape St. Francis D2 32
Cape Town B4 32
Carletonville A1 45
Carlisle Bridge E1 33
Carlow D2 51
Carlsonia E1 43
Carnarvon H3 35
Carolina A1 47
Catembe D1 47
Cathcart B5 38
Catuane C2 47
Cedarville D2 38
Cederberg E5 35
Centani C5 38
Ceres C3 32
Chalumna G1 33
Changalane C1 47
Charl Cilliers D2 45
Charlestown D3 45
Chicabela D1 47
Chicualacuala D1 53
Chipise C1 53
Chrissiesmeer A1 47
Christiana D3 43
Chuniespoort D3 51
Churchhaven A3 32
Ciko D5 38
Cintsa H1 33
Citrusdal E5 35
Clanville B3 38
Clanwilliam E5 35
Clarens C4 45
Clarkebury C4 38
Clarkson C2 32
Clermont G2 39
Clewer D1 45
Clifford B3 38
Clocolan A5 45
Coalville D1 45
Coetzersdam C2 43

Coffee Bay D4 38
Cofimvaba B4 38
Coghlan C4 38
Colekeplaas C2 32
Colenso D4 45
Colesberg D3 37
Coligny E1 43
Committees Drift F1 33
Concordia C1 34
Conway D4 37
Cookhouse E5 37
Copperton A2 36
Corn Exchange C1 38
Cornelia C2 45
Cradock E5 37
Cramond G2 41
Creighton E2 39
Crocodile Bridge D5 53
Croydon C1 47
Cullinan C5 51
Dabenoris D1 34
Dagbreek G4 41
Daggaboersnek E5 37
Daleside B1 45
Dalton F1 39
Daniëlskuil B3 42
Dannhauser A3 47
Dargie F1 39
Darling A3 32
Darnall G1 39
Daskop A2 32
Dasville C2 45
Davel D1 45
De Aar C3 37
De Brug E1 36
De Doorns C4 32
De Gracht C1 51
De Hoek B3 32
De Hoop F4 33
De Rust A1 32
De Vlug B2 32
De-Wildt B5 51
Dealesville E4 43
Deelfontein C3 37
Deelpan E1 43
Delareyville D2 43
Delportshoop C4 43
Demistkraal D2 32
Dendron D2 51
Dennilton D5 51
Derby F1 43
Derdepoort H4 49
Despatch D2 32
Devon C1 45
Devonlea D2 43
Dewetsdorp F1 36
Dibeng A3 42
Die Bos F4 35
Diemansputs H2 35
Dingleton A3 42
Dirkiesdorp A2 47
Diti C1 53
Dlolwana B4 47
Donkerpoort E2 37
Donnybrook E2 39
Dordrecht B4 38
Doringbaai D4 34
Doringbos E4 35
Douglas C1 36
Dovesdale F1 43
Driefontein B3 53
Dullstroom B5 53
Dundee A4 47
Dupleston F2 37
Durban G2 39
Durbanville B4 32
Dutlwe E3 49
Dwaalboom A4 51
Dwarskersbos D5 34
Dweshula F3 39
Dysselsdorp A2 32
East London G1 33

Ebende C5 38
Edenburg E1 36
Edendale F2 39
Edenvale B1 45
Edenville B3 45
Eendekuil E5 35
Eksteenfontein B5 40
Elands Height C3 38
Elandsbaai D5 34
Elandsdrift E5 37
Elandskraal A4 47
Elandslaagte D4 45
Elandsputte E1 43
Elgin B4 32
Elim C5 32
Elim Hospital B2 53
Elliot C4 38
Elliotdale D4 38
Ellisras B2 51
Elmeston B3 51
Emangusi D2 47
Embotyi E4 39
Empangeni H1 39
Engcobo C4 38
Ennerdale B1 45
Entumeni G1 39
Erasmia B1 45
Ermelo A2 47
Eshowe G1 39
Estcourt E1 39
Evander C1 45
Evangelina D1 51
Ewbank B1 42
Excelsior F5 43
Ezibeleni F4 37
Faans Grove H2 41
Fairfield C5 32
Faure B4 32
Fauresmith E1 36
Felixton H1 39
Ficksburg B4 45
Firgrove B4 32
Fish Hoek B4 32
Flagstaff E3 39
Florisbad E4 43
Fochville A1 45
Forbes Reef A1 47
Fort Beaufort F1 33
Fort Brown F1 33
Fort Donald E3 39
Fort Hare F1 33
Fort Mistake D4 45
Fort Mtombeni G1 39
Fouriesburg B4 45
Frankfort C2 45
Franklin E2 39
Franschhoek B4 32
Fraserburg H4 35
Frere E1 39
Ga-Modjadji D2 53
Ga-Mopedi B2 42
Ga-Rankuwa B5 51
Gabane G4 49
Gaborone H4 49
Gamoep D2 34
Gansbaai C5 32
Ganskuil A4 51
Ganyesa C1 43
Garies C3 34
Garryowen B4 38
Gege B2 47
Geluk C2 45
Geluksburg D4 45
Gelukspruit F3 41
Gemsbokvlakte C1 43
Gemvale E4 39
Genadendal A2 32
George A2 32
Germiston B1 45
Geysdorp D1 43
Giesenskraal B2 36
Gilead C3 51
Gingindlovu G1 39

Name	Ref	Page
Giyani	C2	53
Gladdeklipkop	D3	51
Glencoe	A4	47
Glenconnor	D1	32
Glenmore Beach	F3	39
Glenrock	B1	38
Glenrock	E5	37
Gloria	D1	45
Gluckstadt	B4	47
Goageb	B2	40
Goba	C1	47
Goedemoed	F2	37
Goedewil	B5	37
Golela	C3	47
Gompies	D4	51
Gomvlei	F2	37
Gonubie Mouth	G1	33
Good Hope	G5	49
Goodhouse	C5	40
Gordon's Bay	B4	32
Gouda	B3	32
Gouritsmond	F5	33
Graaff-Reinet	D5	37
Graafwater	D5	34
Grabouw	B4	32
Grahamstown	F1	33
Granaatboskolk	F2	35
Grasfontein	E1	43
Graskop	C4	53
Gravelotte	C3	53
Gregory	C1	51
Greylingstad	C2	45
Greystone	D1	32
Greyton	C4	32
Greytown	F1	39
Griekwastad	B4	42
Groblersdal	D4	51
Groblershoop	H4	41
Groenriviersmond	C3	34
Groenvlei	A3	47
Groesbeck	C3	51
Grondneus	F3	41
Groot Brakrivier	A2	32
Groot Jongensfontein	E5	33
Groot Marico	H5	49
Grootdrif	E4	35
Grootdrink	G4	41
Grootkraal	A1	32
Grootmis	B1	34
Grootpan	F1	43
Grootspruit	A3	47
Grootvlei	C2	45
Grünau	C3	40
Ha-Magoro	B2	53
Haarlem	B2	32
Haenertsburg	B3	53
Haga-Haga	H1	33
Halcyon Drift	D3	38
Halfweg	F2	35
Hamburg	G1	33
Hammanskraal	B5	51
Hammarsdale	F2	39
Hankey	D2	32
Hanover	C3	37
Hantam	E4	35
Harding	E3	39
Harrisdale	F3	41
Harrismith	C4	45
Hartbeesfontein	F2	43
Hartbeeskop	A1	47
Hartbeespoort	B5	51
Hartswater	D3	43
Hattingspruit	A4	47
Hauptrus	E1	43
Hawston	B5	32
Hectorspruit	D5	53
Heerenlogement	D4	34
Heidelberg	C1	45
Heidelberg	D4	32
Heilbron	B2	45
Heldina	F1	43
Helmeringhausen	A1	40
Helpmekaar	A4	47
Hendrick's Drift	B4	45
Hendrina	D1	45
Hennenman	F3	43
Herbertsdale	E4	33
Hereford	D4	51
Herefords	A1	47
Hermanus	C5	32
Hermansdorings	B3	51
Herold	A2	32
Heroldsbaai	A2	32
Herschel	B3	38
Hertzogville	D3	43
Heydon	D4	37
Hibberdene	F3	39
Higg's Hope	B1	36
Highflats	F2	39
Hildreth Ridge	B2	53
Hillandale	D3	32
Hilton	F1	39
Himeville	E2	39
Hlabisa	C4	47
Hlathikhulu	B2	47
Hlogotlou	D4	51
Hlotse	B5	45
Hluhluwe	C4	47
Hluthi	B3	47
Hobeni	D5	38
Hobhouse	B1	38
Hoedspruit	B4	53
Hofmeyr	E4	37
Hogsback	F5	37
Holbank	A2	47
Holme Park	C4	51
Holy Cross	E3	39
Hondefontein	G5	35
Hondeklipbaai	C2	34
Hoopstad	E3	43
Hopefield	A3	32
Hopetown	C1	36
Hotagterklip	C5	32
Hotazel	A2	42
Hottentotskloof	C3	32
Hout Bay	A4	32
Howick	F1	49
Hukuntsi	B3	48
Humansdorp	D2	32
Hutchinson	B4	36
Idutywa	C5	38
Ifafa Beach	F3	39
Impisi	E3	39
Inanda	G2	39
Indwe	B4	38
Infanta-on-river	D5	32
Ingwavuma	C3	47
Inhaca	D1	47
Isipingo	G2	39
Iswepe	A2	47
Itsoseng	E1	43
Ixopo	E2	39
Izingolweni	E3	39
Izotsha	F3	39
Jacobsdal	D1	36
Jagersfontein	E1	36
Jaght Drift	G1	35
Jambila	A1	47
Jamestown	F3	37
Jan Kempdorp	D3	43
Jansenville	D1	32
Janseput	C2	51
Jeffrey's Bay	D2	32
Joel's Drift	B4	45
Johannesburg	B1	45
Joubertina	C2	32
Jozini	C3	47
Jwaneng	F4	49
KaNyamazane	C5	53
Kaalrug	C1	47
Kaapmuiden	C5	53
Kaapsehoop	C5	53
Kafferrivier	E1	36
Kakamas	F4	41
Kalamare	H1	49
Kalbaskraal	B4	32
Kalkbank	D2	51
Kalkwerf	G4	41
Kameel	D1	43
Kamieberg	D2	34
Kamieskroon	C2	34
Kampersrus	B4	53
Kang	D2	48
Kanoneiland	G4	41
Kanye	G4	49
Kao	D1	38
Karasburg	D3	41
Karatara	A2	32
Kareedouw	C2	32
Karkams	C2	34
Karos	G4	41
Karreeboschkolk	F2	35
Karringmelkspruit	B3	38
Kasouga Road	F2	33
Kathu	A3	42
Kayaseput	H4	49
Keat's Drift	A5	47
Keat's Drift	F1	39
Keetmanshoop	C2	40
Kei Mouth	C5	38
Kei Road	B5	38
Keimoes	F4	41
Kempton Park	B1	45
Kendal	C1	45
Kendrew	C5	37
Kenhardt	G1	35
Kenilworth	D4	43
Kennedy's Vale	B4	53
Kenton On Sea	F2	33
Kestell	C4	45
Kgagodi	B1	51
Kgolong	D3	48
Khabo	B5	45
Khakhea	D4	48
Khubus	B4	40
Kidd's Beach	G1	33
Kimberley	C4	43
King William's Town	G1	33
Kingsburgh	F2	39
Kingscote	E2	39
Kingsley	A3	47
Kinirapoort	D3	38
Kinross	C1	45
Kirkwood	D1	32
Klaarstroom	A1	32
Klawer	D4	34
Klein Drakenstein	B4	32
Klein Letaba	B2	53
Klein Tswaing	C2	43
Kleinmond	B5	32
Kleinpoort	D1	32
Kleinsee	B2	34
Klerksdorp	F2	43
Klerkskraal	A1	45
Klipfontein	D1	32
Klipfontein	D1	45
Klipplaat	C1	32
Kliprand	D3	34
Klipskool	B5	53
Knysna	B2	32
Koedoeskop	B4	51
Koegas	A1	36
Koenong	C1	38
Koffiefontein	D1	36
Koiingnaas	C2	34
Kokstad	E3	39
Kolonyama	C1	38
Komatipoort	D5	53
Komga	C5	38
Kommaggas	C2	34
Kommandokraal	A1	32
Kommetjie	A4	32
Kommissiepoort	B1	38
Koopan-Suid	F2	41
Koosfontein	D2	43
Kopersluit	C1	51
Kopong	G3	49
Koppies	B2	45
Koringberg	B3	32
Koringplaas	G5	35
Kosmos	B5	51
Koster	F1	43
Kotzesrus	C3	34
Koukraal	F2	37
Koutjie	A2	32
Koës	D1	40
Kraaifontein	B4	32
Kraaldorings	E3	33
Kraankuil	C2	37
Kransfontein	C4	45
Kranskop	A5	47
Kranskop	G1	39
Kriel	D1	45
Kromdraai	D1	45
Kroonstad	F3	43
Krugersdorp	B1	45
Kruisfontein	D2	32
Kruisrivier	F3	33
Ku-Mayima	C4	38
Kubung	C2	38
Kubutsa	B2	47
Kuilsrivier	B4	32
Kuruman	B3	32
KwaMashu	G2	39
KwaMbonambi	C4	47
Kwaggaskop	B5	53
Kwamhlanga	C5	51
Kylemore	B4	32
L'Agulhas	C5	32
La Cotte	C3	53
Laaiplek	A3	32
Labera	F5	49
Ladismith	E4	33
Lady Frere	B4	38
Lady Grey	B3	38
Ladybrand	B1	38
Ladysmith	D4	45
Lahlangubo	D3	38
Laingsburg	D3	32
Lambert's Bay	D5	34
Lammerkop	D5	51
Langberg	E3	33
Langdon	C4	38
Langebaan	A3	32
Langehorn	C1	43
Langholm	F1	33
Lavumisa	C3	47
Leandra	C1	45
Lebowakgomo	D3	51
Leeu-Gamka	H5	35
Leeudoringstad	E2	43
Legkraal	D2	51
Lehlohonolo	D2	38
Lehututu	B3	48
Leipoldtville	D5	34
Lekfontein	F1	33
Lekkersing	B1	34
Lekoa	B2	45
Lemoenshoek	D4	32
Lentsweletau	G3	49
Lephepe	G2	49
Letlhakeng	F3	49
Letseng-La-Terae	D1	38
Letsitele	B3	53
Libode	D4	38
Lichtenburg	E1	43
Lidgetton	F1	39
Limburg	C3	51
Lime Acres	B4	42
Linakeng	D1	38
Lindeshof	C4	32
Lindley	B3	45
Lindleyspoort	H5	49
Llandudno	A4	32
Lobamba	B2	47
Lobatse	G4	49
Loch Vaal	B2	45
Lochiel	A1	47
Loerie	D2	32
Loeriesfontein	E3	35
Logageng	D1	43
Lohatlha	A3	42
Lokgwabe	B3	48
Loskop	E1	39
Lothair	A1	47
Louis Trichardt	B2	53
Louisvale	G4	41
Louwna	C2	43
Louwsburg	B3	47
Lower Dikgetlhong	A2	42
Lower Pitseng	A4	38
Loxton	A4	36
Loyengo	B2	47
Luckhoff	D1	36
Lufuta	C4	38
Lulekani	C3	53
Lundean's Nek	C3	38
Luneberg	A3	47
Lusikisiki	E4	39
Lutombe	B1	53
Lutzville	D4	34
Lydenburg	B4	53
Lykso	C2	43
Maartenshoop	B4	53
Maasstroom	C1	51
Mabaalstad	A5	51
Mabaalstad	F1	43
Mabeskraal	A4	51
Mabopane	B5	51
Mabula	B4	51
Machadodorp	A1	47
Machava	D1	47
Macleantown	G1	33
Maclear	C3	38
Madadeni	A3	47
Madiakgama	C1	43
Madibogo	D1	43
Madipelesa	C3	43
Mafeteng	B2	38
Mafikeng	E1	43
Mafube	D2	38
Mafutseni	B2	47
Magaliesburg	B1	45
Magudu	C3	47
Magusheni	E3	39
Mahalapye	A2	51
Mahlabatini	B4	47
Mahlangasi	C3	47
Mahwelereng	C3	51
Makhaleng	C1	38
Makopong	D4	48
Makwate	A2	51
Malaita	D4	51
Malapati	D1	53
Malealea	C2	38
Malelane	D5	53
Maleoskop	D5	51
Malgas	D5	32
Malmesbury	B4	32
Maloma	C2	47
Mamaila	B2	53
Mamates	C1	38
Mamre	B4	32
Mandini	G1	39
Mangeni	A4	47
Manhoca	D2	47
Mankayane	B2	47
Mankweng	D3	51
Manthestad	D3	43
Mantsonyane	C1	38
Manubi	D5	38
Manzini	B2	47
Mapai	D2	53
Mapela	C3	51
Mapumulo	G1	39
Maputo	D1	47
Marakabei	C1	38
Marble Hall	D4	51
Marburg	F3	39
Marchand	F4	41
Margate	F3	39
Maricosdraai	H4	49
Marikana	A5	51
Marite	C4	53
Marken	C2	51

Place	Grid	Page
Markramsdraai	A3	42
Marnitz	C2	51
Marquard	A4	45
Marracuene	D1	47
Martin's Drift	B2	51
Marydale	H1	35
Maseru	C1	38
Mashai	D1	38
Mashashane	D3	51
Masisi	C1	53
Matatiele	D2	38
Matavhelo	C1	53
Mateka	C1	38
Matjiesfontein	D3	32
Matjiesrivier	F3	33
Matlabas	B3	51
Matlala	D3	51
Matlameng	C1	38
Matola	D1	47
Matroosberg	C3	32
Matsaile	C2	38
Mavamba	C2	53
Mazenod Institute	C1	38
Mazeppa Bay	D5	38
Mbabane	A1	47
Mbaswana	D3	47
McGregor	C4	32
Mdantsane	G1	33
Mekaling	B2	38
Melkbosstrand	B4	32
Melmoth	B4	47
Meltonwold	A4	36
Memel	D3	45
Merindol	F1	43
Merweville	H5	35
Mesa	F1	43
Mesklip	C2	34
Messina	B1	53
Methalaneng	D1	38
Mevedja	D1	47
Meyerton	B2	45
Meyerville	D2	45
Mgwali	B5	38
Mhlambanyatsi	B2	47
Mhlosheni	B3	47
Mhlume	C1	47
Mica	C3	53
Middelburg	D1	45
Middelburg	D4	37
Middelpos	F4	35
Middelwit	A4	51
Middleton	E1	33
Midrand	B1	45
Migdol	D2	43
Millvale	A5	51
Milnerton	B4	32
Misty Mount	D4	38
Mkambati	E4	39
Mkuze	C3	47
Mmabatho	G5	49
Mmathethe	G4	49
Moamba	C1	47
Mochudi	H3	49
Moeng	B1	51
Moeswal	H3	41
Mogalakwenastroom	C3	51
Mogapi	B1	51
Mogapinyana	B1	51
Mogwase	A5	51
Mohales Hoek	B2	38
Mokamole	C3	51
Mokhotlong	D1	38
Mokopung	C2	38
Molepolole	G3	49
Moletsane	C1	38
Moloporivier	E5	49
Molteno	F4	37
Mont Pelaan	D3	45
Montagu	D4	32
Monte Christo	B2	51
Mooifontein	A1	40
Mooifontein	E1	43
Mooirivier	F1	39
Moordkuil	C4	42
Moorreesburg	B3	32
Morgan's Bay	H1	33
Morgenzon	D2	45
Morija	B1	38
Morokweng	B1	42
Morristown	B4	38
Mortimer	E5	37
Morwamosu	D3	48
Moshaneng	G4	49
Moshesh's Ford	C3	38
Mosita	D1	43
Mosopo	G4	49
Mossel Bay	A2	32
Mossel Bay	F4	33
Mossiesdal	D5	51
Motetema	D4	51
Mothae	D1	38
Mothibistat	B2	42
Motokwe	D3	48
Motsiteng	D1	38
Mount Ayliff	E3	39
Mount Fletcher	D3	38
Mount Frere	D3	38
Mount Rupert	C3	43
Mount Stewart	C1	32
Moyeni	C2	38
Mpemvana	A3	47
Mpendle	E1	39
Mpetu	C5	38
Mphaki	C2	38
Mpharane	C2	38
Mpolweni	F1	39
Mpumalanga	F2	39
Mqanduli	D4	38
Mt. Moorosi	C2	38
Mtonjaneni	B4	47
Mtubatuba	C4	47
Mtunzini	H1	39
Mtwalume	F3	39
Muden	A5	47
Muden	F1	39
Muizenberg	B4	32
Mulati	C3	53
Munster	F3	39
Murraysburg	C4	37
Nababeep	C1	34
Nabies	E4	41
Naboomspruit	C4	51
Namaacha	C1	47
Namakgale	C3	53
Namies	E1	35
Napier	C5	32
Nariep	C3	34
Narubis	C2	40
Nature's Valley	B2	32
Ncanara	E2	33
Ncora	C4	38
Ndumo	C2	47
Ndundulu	B4	47
Ndwedwe	G1	39
Neilersdrift	G4	41
Nelspoort	B4	36
Nelspruit	C5	53
New Hanover	F1	39
Newcastle	D3	45
Newington	D4	53
Newsel Beach	G2	39
Ngobeni	B3	47
Ngome	B3	47
Ngonini	A1	47
Ngqeleni	D4	38
Ngqungqu	D4	38
Nhlangano	B2	47
Nhlazatshe	B4	47
Niekerkshoop	B1	36
Nietverdiend	H4	49
Nieu-Bethesda	D4	37
Nieuwoudtville	E4	35
Nigel	C1	45
Nigramoep	C1	34
Nkambak	B3	53
Nkandla	B4	47
Nkau	C2	38
Nkomo	C2	53
Nobantu	D4	38
Nobokwe	C4	38
Noenieput	E3	41
Nohana	C2	38
Noll	A2	32
Nondweni	A4	47
Nongoma	B3	47
Noordhoek	A4	32
Noordkuil	D5	34
Noordoewer	B4	40
Normandien	D3	45
Northam	A4	51
Notintsila	D4	38
Nottingham Road	E1	39
Noupoort	D3	37
Nqabara	D5	38
Nqabeni	E3	39
Nqamakwe	C5	38
Nqutu	A4	47
Nsoko	C2	47
Ntibane	D4	38
Ntseshe	C5	38
Ntshilini	E4	39
Ntywenke	D3	38
Nulli	C1	53
Nuwerus	D3	34
Nylstroom	C4	51
Nyokana	D5	38
Obobogorab	E2	41
Odendaalsrus	F3	43
Ofcolaco	B3	53
Ogies	C1	45
Ohrigstad	B4	53
Okiep	C1	34
Old Bunting	D4	38
Old Morley	D4	38
Olifantshoek	A3	42
Olyfberg	B3	53
Onderstedorings	G2	35
Ons Hoop	B2	51
Onseepkans	D4	40
Ontmoeting	G2	41
Oorwinning	B2	53
Oosdam	E4	33
Oostermoed	A4	51
Orania	C1	36
Oranjefontein	B2	51
Oranjemund	A4	40
Oranjerivier	C1	36
Oranjeville	B2	45
Orkney	F2	43
Osborn	B4	47
Osizweni	A3	47
Ottosdal	E2	43
Oudtshoorn	A2	32
Oukraal	C5	32
Overyssel	B2	51
Oviston	E3	37
Owendale	B4	42
Oxbow	C4	45
Oyster Bay	D2	32
Paarl	B4	32
Pacaltsdorp	A2	32
Paddock	F3	39
Pafuri	D1	53
Palala	C3	51
Palapye	A1	51
Palm Beach	F3	39
Palmerton	E4	39
Palmietfontein	B2	38
Pampierstad	C3	43
Panbult	A2	47
Pansdrif	B5	51
Papendorp	D4	34
Papiesvlei	C5	32
Papkuil	B4	42
Park Rynie	F2	29
Parow	B4	32
Parys	A2	45
Patensie	D2	32
Paternoster	A3	32
Paterson	E1	33
Patlong	C2	38
Paul Roux	B4	45
Paulpietersburg	B3	47
Pearly Beach	C5	32
Pearston	D5	37
Peddie	F1	33
Peka	C1	38
Pella	E1	35
Penge	B4	53
Pennington	F3	39
Perdekop	D2	45
Petersburg	D5	37
Petrus Steyn	B3	45
Petrusburg	E1	36
Petrusville	D2	37
Phalaborwa	C3	53
Phamong	C2	38
Philadelphia	B4	32
Philippolis	D2	37
Philipstown	C2	37
Phitshane Molopo	G5	49
Phokwane	D4	51
Phuthaditjhaba	C4	45
Pienaarsrivier	B4	51
Piet Plessis	C1	43
Piet Retief	B2	47
Pietermaritzburg	F2	39
Pietersburg	D3	51
Piggs Peak	A1	47
Piketberg	B3	32
Pilgrim's Rest	C4	53
Pinetown	F2	39
Pitseng	C1	38
Platbakkies	D2	34
Plathuis	D4	32
Platrand	D2	45
Plettenberg Bay	B2	32
Plooysburg	C5	43
Pniel	B4	32
Pofadder	E1	35
Politsi	B3	53
Pomeroy	A4	47
Pongola	C3	47
Ponta Do Ouro	D2	47
Port Alfred	F2	33
Port Beaufort	D5	32
Port Edward	F3	39
Port Elizabeth	E2	33
Port Grosvenor	E4	39
Port Nolloth	B1	34
Port Shepstone	F3	39
Port St. Johns	E4	39
Porterville	B3	32
Post Chalmers	D4	37
Postmasburg	A4	42
Potfontein	C2	37
Potchefstroom	F2	43
Potgietersrus	C3	51
Potsdam	G1	33
Pretoria	B5	51
Prieska	A1	36
Prince Albert	F3	33
Prince Albert Road	E3	33
Prince Alfred Hamlet	C3	32
Pringle Bay	B5	32
Protem	C5	32
Qabane	C2	38
Qacha's Nek	D2	38
Qamata	B4	38
Qobong	C2	38
Qoboqobo	C5	38
Qolora Mouth	C5	38
Qoqodala	F4	37
Qora Mouth	D5	38
Qudeni	A4	47
Queensburgh	G2	39
Queenstown	F4	37
Quiba	C4	38
Quko	C5	38
Qumbu	D3	38
Radium	C4	51
Ralebona	C2	38
Raleqheka	C1	38
Ramabanta	C1	38
Ramotswa	G4	39
Ramsgate	F3	39
Ranaka	G4	49
Randalhurst	B4	47
Randburg	B1	45
Randfontein	B1	45
Rankin's Pass	A4	51
Rawsonville	C4	32
Rayton	C5	51
Redcliffe	E1	39
Reddersburg	F1	36
Redelinghuys	D5	34
Redoubt	E3	39
Reebokrand	D2	37
Reitz	C3	45
Reitzburg	A2	45
Reivilo	C3	43
Renosterspruit	F2	43
Ressano Garcia	D5	53
Restvale	B4	36
Rex	A5	51
Richards Bay	H1	39
Richmond	C4	37
Richmond	F2	39
Riebeeckstad	F3	43
Riebeek-Kasteel	B3	32
Riebeek-Oos	E1	33
Riebeek-Wes	B3	32
Rietbron	B1	32
Rietfontein	E2	41
Rietkolk	D3	51
Rietkuil	C3	45
Rietpoort	D3	34
Rietvlei	F1	39
Rita	D3	51
Ritchie	C5	43
Riversdale	E4	33
Riverview	C4	47
Riviersonderend	C4	32
Roamer's Rest	D2	38
Robert's Drift	C2	45
Robertson	C4	32
Rode	D3	38
Rodenbeck	F1	36
Roedtan	D4	51
Roma	C1	38
Roodebank	C2	45
Roodepoort	B1	45
Rooiberg	B4	51
Rooibokkraal	A3	51
Rooibosbult	A3	51
Rooigrond	E1	43
Rooikraal	D5	51
Rooipan	D1	36
Rooiwal	A2	45
Roosboom	D4	45
Roossenekal	B5	53
Rorke's Drift	A4	47
Rosebank	F2	39
Rosedene	A4	36
Rosendal	B4	45
Rosetta	E1	39
Rosh Pinah	A3	40
Rosmead	D4	37
Rossouw	B3	38
Rostrataville	E2	43
Rouxpos	E3	33
Rouxville	F2	37
Ruitersbos	C4	32
Rust de Winter	C4	51
Rustenburg	A5	51
Rusverby	H5	49
Ruthmere	D5	38
Saaifontein	H4	35
Sabie	C4	53
Sada	F5	37
Salajwe	F2	49
Salamanga	D2	47
Saldanha	A3	32
Salem	F1	33
Salt Lake	C1	36

Name	Grid	Page
Salt Rock	G1	39
Saltpeterpan	C2	43
Sand River Valley	D4	45
Sandton	B1	45
Sandvlakte	C2	32
Sannieshof	E1	43
Sasolburg	B2	45
Sauer	B3	32
Scarborough	B5	32
Scheepmoor	A2	47
Schweizer Reneke	D2	43
Scottburgh	F2	39
Sea Park	F3	39
Seaview	D2	32
Sebapala	C2	38
Sebayeng	D3	51
Secunda	D2	45
Sedgefield	A2	32
Seekoegat	A1	32
Sefako	C4	45
Sefikeng	C1	38
Sefophe	B1	51
Sehonghong	C2	38
Sekhukhune	B4	53
Sekoma	E3	49
Selonsrivier	D5	51
Sendelingsdrif	A4	40
Sendelingsfontein	E2	43
Sending	D2	51
Senekal	B4	45
Sengwe	C1	53
Senlac	E5	49
Sentrum	A3	51
Seringkop	C5	51
Serowe	A1	51
Seshego	D3	51
Setlagole	D1	43
Settlers	C4	51
Setuat	C2	43
Sevenoaks	F1	39
Severn	A1	42
Seweweekspoort	E3	33
Seymour	F5	37
Sezela	F3	39
Shaka's Rock	G1	39
Shakaskraal	G1	39
Shannon	F1	36
Sheffield Beach	G1	39
Shelly Beach	F3	39
Sherwood Ranch	B2	51
Shoshong	H2	49
Sicunusa	B2	47
Sidvokodvo	B2	47
Sidwadweni	D4	38
Sigoga	D2	38
Sihhoye	C1	47
Sikwane	H4	49
Silent Valley	A3	51
Silkaatskop	H4	49
Silutshana	A4	47
Simon's Town	B5	32
Sinksabrug	A2	32
Sir Lowry's Pass	B4	32
Sishen	A3	42
Siteki	C2	47
Sithobela	C2	47
Sittingbourne	G1	33
Siyabuswa	C4	51
Skipskop	D5	32
Skuinsdrif	H5	49
Slurry	G5	49
Smithfield	F2	37
Smitskraal	C2	32
Sneeukraal	A4	36
Sneezewood	E2	39
Soebatsfontein	C2	34
Soekmekaar	B2	53
Sojwe	G2	49
Somerset East	E5	37
Somerset West	B4	32
Somkele	C4	47
Sonop	B5	51
Sonstraal	H2	41
Southbroom	F3	39
Southeyville	B4	38
Southport	F3	39
Southwell	F2	33
Soutpan	B5	51
Soutpan	E4	43
Soweto	B1	45
Spanwerk	A3	51
Spes Bona	F2	43
Spitskopvlei	D4	37
Spoegrivier	C2	34
Spring Valley	F5	37
Springbok	C1	34
Springfontein	E2	37
Springs	C1	45
St. Faiths	F3	39
St. Francis Bay	D2	32
St. Helena Bay	D5	34
St. Lucia Estuary	C4	47
St. Marks	B4	48
St. Martin	D1	38
Staansaam	F2	31
Stafford's Post	E3	39
Standerton	D2	45
Stanford	C5	32
Stanger	G1	39
Steekdorings	C2	43
Steelpoort	B4	53
Steilrand	B3	47
Steilwater	C2	51
Steinkopf	C1	34
Stella	D1	43
Stellenbosch	B4	32
Sterkspruit	B3	38
Sterkstroom	F4	37
Sterkwater	C3	51
Sterling	H3	35
Steynsburg	E3	37
Steynsrus	A3	45
Steytlerville	C1	32
Still Bay East	E5	33
Still Bay West	E5	33
Stockpoort	A2	51
Stoffberg	D5	51
Stofvlei	D2	34
Stompneusbaai	A3	32
Stoneyridge	D4	38
Stormsrivier	C2	32
Stormsvlei	C4	32
Straatsdrif	H5	49
Strand	B4	32
Strandfontein	D4	34
Struisbaai	C5	32
Strydenburg	C2	37
Studtis	C1	32
Stutterheim	B5	38
Summerstrand	E2	33
Sun City	A5	51
Sunland	E1	33
Sutherland	G5	35
Sutton	A2	42
Suurbraak	D4	32
Swaershoek	E5	37
Swart Umfolozi	B3	47
Swartberg	E2	39
Swartkops	E2	33
Swartmodder	F3	41
Swartplaas	F1	43
Swartputs	B3	42
Swartruggens	H5	49
Swartwater	C1	51
Swellendam	D4	32
Swempoort	B3	38
Swinburne	D4	45
Tabankulu	C1	47
Tabankulu	E3	39
Tainton	H1	33
Takatokwane	D3	49
Taleni	C5	38
Tarkastad	F4	37
Taung	D3	43
Temba	B5	51
Tembisa	B1	45
Terra Firma	D5	48
Teyateyaneng	C1	38
Thaba Bosiu	C1	38
Thaba Chitja	C2	38
Thaba Nchu	F1	36
Thaba Tseka	D1	38
Thabana Morena	B2	38
Thabazimbi	A4	51
Thamaga	G4	49
The Berg	C4	53
The Crags	B2	32
The Downs	B3	53
The Haven	D5	38
The Heads	B2	32
The Ranch	A5	47
The Ranch	G1	39
Theunissen	F4	43
Thohoyandou	C2	53
Thorndale	D2	51
Thornville	F2	39
Tina Bridge	D3	38
Tjaneni	C1	47
Tlali	C1	38
Tlhakgameng	C1	43
Tlokoeng	D1	38
Tlolwe	C2	51
Tom Burke	B2	51
Tombo	E4	39
Tompi Seleka	D4	51
Tonash	C1	51
Tongaat	G2	39
Tontelbos	F3	35
Tosca	C1	43
Tosing	C2	38
Touws River	C3	32
Trawal	D4	34
Trichardt	D2	45
Trichardtsdal	B3	33
Triple Streams	D3	38
Trompsburg	E2	37
Tsatsu	F5	49
Tsazo	C4	38
Tses	C1	40
Tseteng	D2	48
Tsetsebjwe	C1	51
Tshabong	H1	41
Tshakhuma	B2	53
Tshane	B3	48
Tshani	D4	38
Tshani	D4	38
Tshidilamolomo	F5	49
Tshipise	B1	53
Tshiturapadsi	C1	53
Tsineng	A2	42
Tsitsa Bridge	D4	38
Tsoelike	C2	38
Tsolo	D4	38
Tsomo	C5	38
Tugela Ferry	A4	47
Tugela Mouth	G1	39
Tulbagh	B3	32
Twee Rivieren	F1	41
Tweefontein	E5	35
Tweeling	C3	45
Tweespruit	B1	38
Tyira	D3	38
Tylden	B5	38
Tzaneen	B3	53
Ubombo	C3	47
Ugie	C3	38
Uitenhage	D2	32
Uitkyk	D2	34
Uitspankraal	E4	35
Ulco	C4	43
Ulundi	B4	47
Umbogintwini	G2	39
Umbumbulu	F2	39
Umdloti Beach	G2	39
Umhlanga	G2	39
Umkomaas	F2	39
Umlazi	G2	39
Umtata	D4	38
Umtentu	E4	39
Umtentweni	F3	39
Umzimkulu	E2	39
Umzinto	F2	39
Umzumbe	F3	39
Underberg	E2	39
Uniondale	B2	32
Upington	G4	41
Usutu	C1	51
Utrecht	A3	47
Uvongo	F3	39
Vaalhoek	C4	53
Vaalplaas	C5	51
Vaalwater	B3	51
Val	C2	45
Van Reenen	D4	45
Van Rooyen	A4	47
Van Wyksdorp	E4	33
Van Wyksvlei	H2	35
Van Zylsrus	H2	41
Vanalphensvlei	C3	51
Vanderbijlpark	B2	45
Vanderkloof	D2	37
Vandyksdrif	D1	45
Vanrhynsdorp	D4	34
Vanstadensrus	B2	38
Vant's Drift	A4	47
Vegkop	B3	45
Velddrif	A3	32
Ventersburg	F3	43
Ventersdorp	F1	43
Venterskroon	A2	45
Venterstad	E3	37
Vereeniging	B2	45
Verena	C5	51
Vergeleë	E5	49
Verkykerskop	D3	45
Vermaaklikheid	E5	33
Vermaas	E1	43
Verulam	G2	39
Verwoerdburg	B1	45
Victoria West	B4	36
Viedgesville	D4	38
Vier-en-Twintig Riviere	C3	51
Vierfontein	F2	43
Viljoensdrif	B2	45
Viljoenshof	C5	32
Viljoenskroon	F2	43
Villa Nora	B2	51
Villiers	C2	45
Villiersdorp	C4	32
Vineyard	F3	37
Vioolsdrif	B4	40
Virginia	F3	43
Vivo	D2	51
Vleesbaai	F5	33
Vleiland	E3	33
Volksrust	D3	45
Volop	H4	41
Volstruisleegte	B1	32
Voortrekkerspos	A3	51
Vorstershoop	D5	48
Vosburg	B2	36
Vrede	C3	45
Vredefort	A2	45
Vredenburg	A3	32
Vredendal	D4	34
Vredeshoop	E2	41
Vroeggedeel	H3	41
Vrouenspan	F3	41
Vryburg	C2	43
Vryheid	A3	47
Vundica	D1	47
Waenhuiskrans	D5	32
Wagenaarskraal	A4	36
Wakkerstroom	A3	47
Walkerville	B1	45
Wallekraal	C2	34
Wanda	C1	51
Warburton	A1	47
Warmbad	C4	51
Warmbad	D4	40
Warmfontein	D2	40
Warmwaterberg	D4	32
Warrenton	D3	43
Wasbank	A4	47
Waterford	D1	32
Waterkloof	D2	37
Waterpoort	D2	51
Waterval-Boven	B5	53
Wavecrest	C5	38
Waverley	A1	45
Weenen	F1	39
Wegdraai	H4	41
Welkom	F3	43
Wellington	B4	32
Welverdiend	A1	45
Wepener	B1	38
Werda	D4	48
Wesley	G1	33
Wesselsbron	E3	43
Wesselsvlei	B2	42
Westerberg	A1	36
Westonaria	B1	45
Weza	E3	39
Whites	F3	43
Whitmore	C4	38
Whittlesea	F5	37
Wiegnaarspoort	B5	36
Wilderness	A2	32
Williston	G4	35
Willowmore	B1	32
Willowvale	C5	38
Winburg	F4	43
Windmill	B4	32
Windsorton	C4	43
Winkelpos	F3	43
Winterton	D5	45
Winterveld	B5	51
Witbank	D1	45
Witdraai	F2	41
Witkop	F3	37
Witnek	C5	51
Witpoort	E2	43
Witput	C1	36
Witpütz	A3	40
Witrivier	C5	53
Witsand	D5	32
Wittedrift	B2	32
Witteklip	D2	32
Witwater	D2	34
Wolmaransstad	E2	43
Wolseley	B3	32
Wolvepoort	F2	37
Wolwefontein	D1	32
Wolwehoek	B2	45
Wolwespruit	D4	43
Wondermere	H5	49
Woodlands	C2	32
Wooldridge	G1	33
Worcester	C4	32
Woudkop	C2	51
Wuppertal	E5	35
Wydgeleë	D5	32
Wyford	D4	45
Xolobe	C5	38
Yzerfontein	A3	32
Zaaimansdal	B2	32
Zastron	B2	38
Zebediela	D3	51
Zeerust	H5	49
Zitundo	D2	47
Zoar	E4	33
Zunckels	D5	45
Zwartkop	G2	35
Zwelitsha	G1	33
Zwingli	H4	49